IRMA

Also by Terry McDonell

The Accidental Life: An Editor's Notes on Writing and Writers

Wyoming: The Lost Poems

California Bloodstock

IRMA

THE EDUCATION OF A MOTHER'S SON

TERRY McDONELL

HARPER

An Imprint of HarperCollins*Publishers*

IRMA. Copyright © 2023 by Robert T. McDonell. All rights reserved. Printed in the United States of America. No part of this book may be used or reproduced in any manner whatsoever without written permission except in the case of brief quotations embodied in critical articles and reviews. For information, address Harper-Collins Publishers, 195 Broadway, New York, NY 10007.

HarperCollins books may be purchased for educational, business, or sales promotional use. For information, please email the Special Markets Department at SP-sales@harpercollins.com.

FIRST EDITION

Library of Congress Cataloging-in-Publication Data has been applied for.

ISBN 978-0-06-327797-7

23 24 25 26 27 LBC 5 4 3 2 1

Single mothers
Fatherless sons
&
For my sister
Cheryl Noreen Elden Kirby
Irma's daughter

Proem

I gave birth to a son, and he shot up equal to a seedling. I nurtured him like a shoot in the choicest spot of the orchard, only to send him off on curved ships to Troy, to fight Trojan men.

—LAMENT OF THETIS, *The Iliad* (18.52–64), HOMER

Every life is in many days, day after day. We walk through ourselves, meeting robbers, ghosts, giants, old men, young men, wives, widows, brothers-in-love, but always meeting ourselves.

—*Ulysses*, JAMES JOYCE

Part I

...

FIGHTER PILOT

1

(AIR STATIONS)

He hated secrets. There were already too many things he did not want to know, and they prowled around in his head long after his innocence was gone and he could speak for himself.

Irma

After Bob goes down, it is just Irma and me. Men notice. I hear them say Irma is a dish. Irma drives a Chevy Club Coupe with a jump seat that folds down flat. Irma likes to drive and sometimes I sleep in the back. We get around.

We move to places where she and Bob lived when he was a fighter pilot. There is always an Air Station, like the US Naval Air Station at Norfolk, where I was born. After Norfolk we live in Memphis, and then Gulf Breeze, which is part of Pensacola. I have no memory of Norfolk or Memphis or Pensacola, although I have been back to look at them. They mean nothing to me now.

Irma went to college and gets to be a schoolteacher anywhere she wants, like Orange, Texas. She never lived there with Bob, but there is an Air Station, and she knows some of the pilots from when Bob was not dead. Orange is where I start remembering things, like my first cowboy boots, which Irma gives me on Easter Sunday, the same day I get my first bee sting. I have a photograph. I am in my boots, with shorts and kid suspenders. That is all I am wearing.

I am playing on the lawn and the bee gets me on my knee. I run to our porch and one of Irma's friends from the Air Station pulls apart one of his Chesterfields and tapes the tobacco on my sting.

He says it will fix me right up, and it does. I do not remember his name, which is not right because he sleeps over sometimes and we roughhouse before I go to bed. He tells me clover is coming up on the lawn or there would not be any bees. I remember that too, just not his name.

When Irma gets tired of Texas, we drive the Chevy back to Minnesota to live with Nana and Pops in Duluth, where Irma and Bob fell for each other. The house is on High Street, and has a long porch across the front. Irma says this is where Bob was a little boy, and shows me how you can see Lake Superior from the porch.

As soon as we get inside and stop hugging each other, Nana looks at my cowboy boots and tells Irma they will ruin my feet. I make up how I am pretty sure Bob had cowboy boots. Everybody laughs, and I think Irma will say it is okay for me to have my boots, but Nana takes them off me and puts them away, like we never even lived in Orange, Texas. When I start to cry, Pops tells me Bob never cried.

On Saturdays, we drive out to Grandma and Grandpa's farm in Solon Springs, where Irma was a little girl. Irma calls her mother Fronie, which is short for Sophronia, so I call her Fronie too. My grandpa is just Grandpa. They have a cow named Bossy the Cow and chickens that I like, and an old dog that never wants to play. Fronie bakes bread. The room where I sleep with Irma has tiny rosebuds all over the walls. When I lie down for my nap, I wonder how many there are, but I cannot count that high.

Grandpa has a workshop in a shed next to the barn, and he makes a bench for me to sit on in the back of Irma's Chevy. I want to help because it is my bench, but when I ask him if I can hammer the nails, he shakes his head, which means I am supposed to be quiet. Or maybe he does not like me much.

When I tell Fronie how my Nana made Irma take my cowboy boots away, she looks at me funny and I think I have done something wrong. Fronie says, "She's the one with the money." I do not know what that means. Or maybe I do. Later, I hear her talking to Grandpa. Fronie says it is not good for a boy to be raised only by women. She tells him to pay more attention to me, but he does not have time.

Nana gives me a cowboy hat to make up for my boots and then hugs me. I say I do not want the hat because I cannot be a cowboy without my boots and she hugs me harder and then lets go fast. Irma says I can be a cowboy later. Pops tells me I am the man of the family now, so I must take good care of Irma. I have heard that before, but I do not know how to take care of Irma. I tighten myself. No more crying. Nana says I am just like Bob, and I believe her.

I can say Nana's phone number. Hemlock-142. I am cute like that. Pops teaches me how to ask grown-up questions when his friends come over, like "How about a highball?" Sometimes they pull nickels out of my ears. I sit on Pops's lap and listen to them talk about the war. Pops likes to talk about my uncle Jack, who is Bob's younger brother and a pilot too. Pops says Jack is just like Bob except he bombed the Nazis in France. Jack got shot down on a night mission but was such a good pilot he made a crash landing. That was how he saved his crew.

I like the story Jack always tells about when he finally comes home from the war to the house on High Street and I am a year old and he is in his uniform and smoking a cigar and it is the first time he sees me and he picks me up and tosses me over his head with his arms up to catch me but on my way down he puts his cigar out on my forehead. Jack knew right then that we were going to get along because I did not cry. Sometimes people listening to Jack give each other looks like maybe he is fooling, but they do not know anything.

Irma does not like stories about the war because people die, like Bob. Pops never talks about Bob, but Irma always stays in the kitchen with Nana and Nana's friends, who talk about how the war is over and what they did when they found out. One night, when Irma is tucking me in, I ask her what we did. She says we drove downtown in Duluth, where people were riding around honking their horns. Then we just came home. Irma says I will understand when I'm not a little boy anymore.

I see Irma is sad, which makes me think about Bob. I make up a story about how Bob shot down a hundred Jap Zeros before they got him. We sneak up to Nana's attic, where there is a trunk of Bob's uniforms. Irma shows them to me and says we are going to move again. "California," she whispers because it is a secret. She hands me a leather case with Bob's wings and ribbon bars inside.

"California," Irma says again, and hugs me. "We'll take good care of each other."

I turn Bob's wings over in my hands.

Buckaroo

Irma buys a new Ford convertible so we can drive to California with the top down. It is a color nobody has heard of called maroon, which I say is my new favorite color. I have my own suitcase and Irma lets me bring the bench I made with my Grandpa. Bob's trunk is not coming with us, but we are going to send for it. Irma puts suntan lotion on me because we are working on our tans. We eat at drive-ins and stay in motels. Every morning Irma tells me where we were going to stop for the night.

"Cheyenne, Wyoming," she says, on the third morning. "They have a rodeo." Irma pulls my cowboy hat out of her bag and I put it on and she takes a picture with her Brownie camera to send to Nana. When we get to Cheyenne, Irma parks in front of a cowboy store with rodeo posters in the window. We go inside and I pick out boots with six-shooters on them. I am thinking I need a cap gun, but Irma and I have talked about how I must be six to have a cap gun, and I am only four.

Our motel has a neon sign with a bronc buster waving his hat over the gravel entrance. Maybe I will be a bronc buster too, because I have my boots and hat on, with shorts and suspenders like in Texas. I follow Irma into the office, where a woman with piled-up hair and a scarf around her neck is behind a high desk. Next to her in a stuffed chair is a man smoking a cigarette under a big cowboy hat. Next to the man is a boy maybe a year older than me eating out of a box of Cheerios with his pudgy fists. He stares at me, and I stand close to Irma while she signs us in.

The boy is wearing boots that are brown and scuffed, and bib-front overalls with no T-shirt. The man in the chair nudges him forward, and the boy holds out the box of cereal to me. When I reach to take it, he pulls it back and punches me in the stomach. I bend over and roll onto the floor, but I do not cry.

"I guess my boy don't care much for little dudes," the man says, and then laughs a loud bark.

Irma picks me up and carries me to the car and we find our room, where we sit on the bed. Irma says the rodeo will still be fun. I do not want to go, but Irma says we are going and makes me wear my boots and hat. We find our seats in the grandstand and a guy who I can tell is a real cowboy turns around and tells Irma it looks like she has a tough little buckaroo there, and she tells him he has that right. I like how Irma and the cowboy are getting along so good. I like the rodeo too, and at the end they have fireworks, which I have never seen before.

Back at the motel I flop down on the bed and Irma sits next to me and rubs my back. She says she is proud of me and I pretend to fall asleep. She takes off my boots and puts a blanket over me. Pretty soon, she gets up and I hear the door open and close. I know she will be right back, but I listen for her in the darkness until light is coming through the window.

"Salt Lake City," Irma says, when we get in the Ford that morning. "Maybe we'll meet some Mormons." She is kind of laughing, like there's something funny about Mormons. She tells me that if I were a Mormon I could have as many wives as I wanted. I know it is a joke, but I do not get it.

We listen to the car radio all day. Irma's favorite song is "Que Sera Sera" by Doris Day. I want to know why and she says because it is pretty and true at the same time. We go over the words, about how the future is not ours to see because whatever will be will be.

We do not meet any Mormons in Salt Lake City because we only stop at a gas station with souvenirs. Irma buys me a postcard with a little bag of salt sewn onto a picture of the lake.

We keep driving.

Irma says we are going to pick up the pace, which makes me happy. We are hopeful in ways that promise transformation, although I do not think like that then. Irma will teach school and have a new life without Bob. I will be exactly like Bob except I will wear my cowboy boots. I lie down in the back seat and think about that kid back at the motel. I can see the future, or part of it anyway: the part where I never let any kid beat me up because I am a tough buckaroo fighter pilot. Sometimes I suck on that little bag of salt.

We drive all night. I wake up when we stop for gas. Elko, Reno, Sacramento, and then it is morning and we are at a motel on the El Camino Real in Santa Clara.

Norm is waiting for us.

2

(THE VALLEY)

He did not think about growing up. He thought about where he lived, and lived there in real time until things happened that made him think about the future. These things did not change the trees or the birds or the other things he liked. He was never tired, unyielding, although he did not yet understand that came from his mother.

Norm

Norm is tall and thin like a rake handle. He knew Irma and Bob when they were young together. I do not know that when I meet Norm, but I figure it out later, like I figure out a lot of things. Irma tells me Norm was in the war like Bob, except not a fighter pilot. She hugs me and says we are a family with Norm now.

We live at the motel. I sleep on a cot Irma makes into a bed for me. She and Norm pencil circles in the classifieds every morning. When they go out, I stay at the motel. I am the only kid there, but the owners have a scotty dog they call Scotty that they let me play with sometimes. Irma comes back and reads to me every afternoon, which is my favorite time. The rest is just time.

Norm says we are pals and gives me an insignia patch from the Persian Gulf Command. He says he wore it in lots of battles, but it is stiff and feels new. I like it anyway because it has a white star and a red sword. Norm tells me the sword is a scimitar, that the ancient Persians used to chop heads, heads my age, even baby heads. The star is from the Kingdom of Iraq, which he says has a stupid religion that makes you go to hell if you look at women. Norm says it was hot as hell there and he drove bulldozers and Caterpillar tractors with bullet shields and built airstrips. After that, he was in Venezuela, which he will tell me about when I am older. Norm says now that he is in California, he is going to build subdivisions, which is what he is planning when he sits on the motel porch and drinks beers and smokes his Chesterfields, like the guy in Texas.

One afternoon, Irma tells me we are going to leave early the next morning, but we cannot tell the people who own the motel because it will hurt their feelings. Norm asks me if I can keep a secret. I can because I like the motel people and their Scotty, and I do not want to hurt their feelings. Irma wakes me up in the dark and carries me to the car. I remember it was a secret that we were coming to California.

Dogpatch

We move to another motel and then another before we move to a house with a tarpaper roof in Willow Glen, which is an old neighborhood in San Jose. Irma says she is happy to be in a real house, but not in the part of Willow Glen that does not have sidewalks. When Norm and Irma talk about it, she says we live in Dogpatch. Norm says it is a teardown and what does she expect.

Norm gets mad when it rains because there is no construction work for him. Irma wants to be a substitute teacher, but it takes time to get into the system. Sometimes I have Cheerios for dinner, which is fine with me because I do not like the SPAM Norm eats.

At Christmas, all the houses on some of the streets in Willow Glen have the same size Christmas tree with red and green lights in their front yards. Rich people even cover their houses with lights, which Norm says is a waste of electricity. We do not get a tree until Christmas Eve, when Norm tells me they are free from the tree lots. Irma drives us to one of the lots and we wait in the car while Norm jumps out with the engine running and grabs a tree. We drive home down the blocks with lighted trees. When I am older, I think of those streets when I am landing at small airports.

Fort

There is a field overgrown with tall grass behind our house. Irma walks me to our back fence and asks me if I see what a beautiful field it is, which I do. She says I will be allowed to play there when I am home alone if I promise to be careful not to get lost. I promise. I always do what Irma says, but maybe I was going to play in the field anyway because I do not have any kids to play with and Bob would understand. Irma says maybe I can build my own fort.

I climb the fence every day, even in the rain. No one but me is ever there. I walk all the way around the fence line. Sometimes I count my steps. At the far end of the field there is a house where kids live and I watch them, but I do not know them and they never see me. Maybe I am a sniper. Sometimes I crawl through the grass, sneaking up because I am fighting for America. I know all about it because of Bob. For my fort, I dig a trench in the damp earth and cover it with loose boards I find along the fence. Sometimes I sit in my fort until it is time to go home for dinner. I see the light change. I wait for it to get dark. I will always have a fort.

Seacliff

Norm's dad, Adolph, comes to visit. He brings us a silver ashtray with *Norge* stamped on the bottom that he bought on his trip back to Norway, where he was born. Norm says Adolph taught him how to be a ski jumper when he was growing up in Duluth. Nobody says anything about Norm's mom. Adolph sleeps in my bedroom, and I sleep on the couch. Adolph has trouble getting around, so he sits in our best chair all day. He never says anything when I am alone with him. He just looks at me like he does not even know who I am.

Norm wants to take Adolph for a picnic at the beach, so Irma sits in the back with me, and Norm drives us to Seacliff State Beach. It is cold, with a rainy wind, but we eat sandwiches at a picnic table that has people's initials carved into it. Norm and Irma have beers. Adolph asks Irma for coffee but Irma did not bring any. Norm starts complaining about his boss, who does not like him because he is smarter than the boss. I can see Irma does not like this. Then Norm tells Adolph to tell everyone back in Duluth that he and Irma took him for a picnic on the beach in February.

"Tell them that's what it's like in California," he says. Adolph nods. Norm puts his arm around Irma, "Tell them the prettiest girl in Duluth is with me now." Adolph gives me one of his looks.

IRMA

When Adolph goes back to Duluth, Irma tells me not to worry because I will not have to take care of her when she is old. I know I am never going to see Adolph again, just like I know we are never going to be rich like Norm says. I am not worried, though, because *que sera sera . . .*

Private Property

Spring comes, and the field behind our house turns brown as the grasses dry out. I see a small woodpile close to my fort that was hidden by the winter grass. I already know the word *camouflage*, so I rub dirt on my face as I crawl up to the woodpile, which is a Nazi pillbox.

After I kill the Nazis and take the pillbox, I turn over one of the boards and see hundreds of earwigs and ants and other insects I do not know. I look closely and see that some of them are caught in spiderwebs. I am careful because I do not want a black widow to get me. Black widows are the most dangerous spiders in the world, and if one bites you, you start itching and your face turns red and swells up and you get cramps all over and you twitch and throw up until you are dead. I do not know how I know about black widows. Maybe Norm told me about them to scare me. Black widows eat their husbands and babies, which also sounds like something he would tell me.

By summer I do not crawl through the grass anymore because it is full of foxtail stickers, and the ground is hard and dusty. The Woodpile War is over, and I won. I am careful to check for black widows, which are one hundred times more poisonous than rattlesnakes. I think how it would be fun to talk to other kids about black widows and rattlesnakes, but I do not know any.

When it is fall, I go to kindergarten at Willow Glen Elementary. Norm has a job building Anderson Dam on the way to Gilroy, which he jokes is the garlic capital of the world and holds his nose. I am interested in the dam, but he and Irma like to talk about buying a house in a better neighborhood. Norm says the field behind this house is a problem because it is the last pasture in Willow Glen and is too small for a subdivision. Otherwise he would buy it.

I do not say the field is my best place to play, but Norm is looking at me like he knows and tells me never to go there because it is private property. I look at Irma but she does not say anything. Norm tells me not to look at Irma when he is talking to me, and I better understand what he is saying. I tell him he is not my dad, which is what I have been thinking since Adolph left, but I feel bad as soon as I say it because I can see it makes Irma sad. She says I should go to my room. Norm comes in later and asks if I want to go to a baseball game sometime.

Sure I do.

Irma

Irma is a substitute teacher now. Norm calls it "substituting" and says there is not enough money in it and she should be a secretary. Irma says she did not go to college to be a secretary. Norm says college is not that important. Irma says the important thing is that she is reliable, so she gets called a lot, usually very early in the morning, when the regular teachers call in sick. On those days, she drops me off at my school on her way. It is always before other kids get there, and I sit on a bench on the playground and wait.

The older kids get to school first, but they do not talk to me because I am too little. I watch them play kickball or chase each other around. I do not really watch—it is more like I am in my fort.

I wonder if Adolph is dead yet.

The Valley of Heart's Delight

We move to a duplex where the grown-ups next door shout at each other and send their three little kids outside to play but they just stand in the driveway and cry. I feel sorry for them, but Norm says I should not even think about them because we are going in the other direction.

We move two more times before we buy a house in Burbank, which is next to San Jose and where the orchards start—cherries and prunes and apricots and peaches, sometimes with giant walnut trees along the edges. Irma and I like the peaches best, but they have the shortest season.

Some of the orchards are going to be subdivisions, so there are empty dirt fields with more foxtails and loose piles of broken trees. Burbank is too old to be a subdivision, and the houses are all different except they are all small. Some of them are new and small, and there are still vacant lots that people buy if they want to build a house the way they want it. Norm says that is stupid. He likes subdivisions.

Irma says the Santa Clara Valley has scenic beauty because of the fruit trees with their pink and orange and white blossoms. Norm jokes that we live in "The Valley of Heart's Delight," which is what it says on a billboard on the El Camino Real. Irma likes the billboard because it has a map of the valley with different fruits painted on it like a postcard. I know Norm means something different from what Irma likes about the billboard because he does not think the orchards are worth looking at until they are subdivisions.

Flu Shot

Some kids at my school get the flu and it is no big deal until we hear a little girl back in Willow Glen is dead because the flu got her. Irma says it is the Asian Flu that comes from birds, which does not make sense to me. Norm says if it was serious they would close the schools. Then they close the schools. I think about the little girl, but I am not thinking about her fever or if her throat hurt when she coughed. I think about having to wait in bed to die.

When we go back to school, a nurse gives all the kids flu shots. Norm says the only good thing about the shots is that they are free. This makes Irma angry. She does not want me to see. I always see.

Eucalyptus

Irma brings schoolbooks home and we sit on the cinder-block step to our backyard and I read along with her. I tell Irma I am going to read every book in the world. She says Bob liked to read too. I can read before all the other kids, but they do not know that. Irma says that is fine because people do not have to know everything to be friends.

There are lots of new kids. They just show up at school one day or I see them riding their bikes on my block. I ask them where they are from and hear Texas and Oklahoma and even Pennsylvania and lots of other states. When they ask me back, I say, "California."

"Where you really from?"

"Here," I say.

If I think they do not believe me, I tell them I might *sock them in the mouth*, is how I say it. Sometimes I hit them without saying anything. That is what I do to Tommy Robertson, but then I tell him the sock is part of becoming friends. I am not the same kid I was in Texas or Duluth or especially Cheyenne, Wyoming, or even that first motel on the El Camino in Santa Clara.

Irma and Norm are different too, working on their own transformations, which I figure out later. Irma says we are lucky we are in California, and double lucky that we found the Santa Clara

Valley. Norm says progress is happening because people drive to California just to see it, like he did, and then stay because the war is over and it is time to get rich. He says this is good for real estate. He tells people he is from California too, because it helps him sell cheap tract houses to families who just got here. He says that is how smart he is.

Irma invents a game for me to name the trees I see out the window when we take Sunday drives with Norm to look at the new subdivisions. I can name all the fruit trees and figs and almonds and walnuts and all the different kinds of oaks. Eucalyptus trees are my favorite, stretching out in tall rows as windbreaks. Irma says they are from Australia, but perfect for California—like us. I like the tall palm trees too, but Norm says rats live in them at the top.

On our way home, Norm and Irma like to stop for beers at The 49er and I wait in the car. Norm always says they will be out in a couple minutes but they never are. If I remember to bring a book, I read. Usually I forget, so I wait in the driver's seat with my hands on the steering wheel, pretending to drive. I turn the steering wheel hard like I am not supposed to do. One time, when Irma brings a hamburger out for me, I ask if I can keep books in the car, and she says she will talk to Norm about it because he does not like messy cars. I start hiding books under the seat. I do not tell Irma.

When Irma and Norm go out at night, I have a babysitter who likes books too and we read together. Sometimes after we read, she likes to lie on the rug and I sit on her butt and bounce up and down. When she asks me to touch her in other places, I do, which is another secret. She touches me sometimes too.

Schwinn Phantom

The neighborhood is flat, from San Jose Los Gatos Road out to the orchards. On one side is Moorpark Avenue, where my school is, and then rows of strawberries and more cherry orchards. On the other side is Stevens Creek Road, with more orchards except where a shopping center is going in. Irma and Norm say it is dangerous for me to play where the construction is because of the giant dirt piles and all the heavy equipment.

I go there anyway, like I go everywhere as soon as I have my bike, which is a Schwinn Phantom that Norm gets me used. I want a new bike, but they are too expensive, and Irma says what something costs does not matter unless you let it. She says I should think about that. So my Phantom is rusted and beat-up, but I do not care because I can pedal faster than any other kid. Irma shows me how to put playing cards on the wheel forks with clothespins so they snap loud in the spokes like when she was a little girl in Solon Springs and rode her bike three miles to school.

All the dogs in the neighborhood chase cars, and sometimes they chase me on my bike. I pedal hard and then lift my feet up. Norm says I should kick them because that is the best way to train a dog. I am never going to kick a dog.

IRMA

———

I have lots of friends now and we all have bikes and ride to the different orchards. We know when the ranchers open the irrigation ditches, and we try to get there to see the water run. It comes fast at first and stays fast, even with the dirt soaking it up. The ranchers walk their ditches in high boots, opening and closing gates to different rows of trees, balancing the water.

We are not allowed to play in the orchards and especially not in the irrigation ditches, but in the summer that is what we do. Mostly we just splash around, but the banks are steep with loose dirt that washes away under us when we climb out. One time I have to pull one of my friends out of the fast water. We are both laughing when I finally get him up on the bank, but we do not swim there anymore.

We dig foxholes and trenches in the vacant lots and have rock fights and lob grass bombs at each other. "Let's play war!" we shout. Sometimes: "Let's play cavalry!" We play cavalry on our bikes, pedaling fast all over the neighborhood until someone shouts, "Let's play Custer!" and we jump off our bikes, cocking our imaginary Winchesters to shoot as many Sioux as we can before we die on our dirt mounds. We all want to be cavalry officers. We all want to die young on a hill.

For my ninth birthday, I want a real cavalry sword and an army pup tent. Norm says he will see about the sword, but they are hard to find and tents are too expensive. I wonder about that because a kid named Calvin, who wears ratty T-shirts and whose dad works construction and knows Norm from the 49er, has a tent and we sleep out in his backyard sometimes. One time his dad comes home late and wakes us up. He pulls back the flap and leans his big head into the tent and says the war might have been fine for some people but it sure as hell wasn't fine for him because he sure as hell is not getting rich.

Calvin does not get it, but I do. When his dad leaves, Calvin pretends like everything is funny and asks me if I would rather be in a war or have a baby. Dumb question.

Starlings

One of my friends gets a BB gun because his dad is a hunter and wants him to be a hunter too. We take turns shooting at different birds—blue jays and robins and crows—but never hit any. Sometimes there are so many starlings flocking over the cherry orchards you cannot see the sky, but we still never hit any. All the kids think it would be more fun to have BB gun wars and shoot at each other, but we only have one gun.

Irma gets me a bird book full of pictures, and I show her all the birds I have seen, which is a lot. She says I should learn all the birds like I am learning the trees. I say there might be too many. She says I should try because the new subdivisions will not be good for the birds and I will want to remember them.

Norm hears us talking and gets mad and says there are so many birds it will not matter, just like me and my friends think when we are shooting at them with the BB gun.

Mexicans

The mom of one of my friends takes us to see *The Little Rascals* at the Burbank Theater for his birthday. I like Spanky and Alfalfa and the rest of them, but they are not like us at all. They have fun all the time and do not have any Mexicans to worry about. We are afraid of Mexicans, even though we do not know any as young as us. When we see their older brothers riding around in their lowrider cars, we know they all have switchblades for gang fights in East San Jose. Norm calls Mexicans *pachucos* or *wetbacks*. Irma says she hates those names. Norm says the *greasers* are all in gangs and their girlfriends have nests of black widows in their ratted hair.

Sometimes I get my friends and we go to an orchard and pick up prunes or apricots off the ground for a nickel a bucket, which is what the Mexicans get. This is hard for us, though, because we follow the Mexicans, who move fast behind the ranchers, who shake the trees with long poles or bump them with their tractors. We pick up whatever the Mexicans miss, but that is not much. We joke around and quit whenever we want, like when we pick enough to buy a six-pack of Royal Crown Cola, which costs a quarter.

One time, I work all day by myself to get seventy-five cents to buy a flashlight so I can read at night under my covers.

The Catcher in the Rye

Irma and Norm have drinks with our new neighbors, Bob and Ginny. I like Bob best because of his name, but I like Ginny too because she is pretty, like Irma. They are from Bucks County, which is back east, but not like where we are from. I do not know why I like it that they drink Manhattans instead of beer, but I do.

Bob and Ginny came to California for Bob's job in an insurance office in San Jose. Ginny went to Ursinus College back in Pennsylvania, and talks about being there with a writer named J. D. Salinger. Irma has read his book, which is called *The Catcher in the Rye*, and says she liked it. I sit on the floor and listen and wait for Bob to give me his maraschino cherry, which he does sometimes, and I taste the liquor on it.

"I don't read anything that's not true," Norm says. "Why should I?"

"To improve your mind," Ginny says.

Norm does not like this and makes a joke about how he would rather improve his bank account, which makes me think about our first motel on the El Camino and those free Christmas trees in Willow Glen.

Redwoods

I am in the Wolf Patrol of Cub Scout Pack 318. Irma is one of the den mothers. We get blue uniforms like Custer's 7th Cavalry had at Little Bighorn. Irma gives me a book called *Custer's Last Stand*, and I like Crazy Horse because he is the best fighter and likes to make plans, like me. Irma says there are more books I will like, and that the Sioux like to be called *Lakota*.

My best friend in Cubs is a shy kid who likes Indians too. His father is a policeman who is building a cabin with his policemen friends in the Santa Cruz Mountains. I get to go there for a weekend, and we play Indians in the forest, which is better than in the orchards. Instead of irrigation ditches there is a creek and even a waterfall. We ambush lots of cavalry in the groves of giant redwoods. My friend's dad says some of the trees are from way before anybody came to America.

I tell Irma about the redwoods. I say how old they are, and she tells me there were lots of different people in America a long time before people like us got here, and she will bring home a book about that for me. It is a picture book, and I will like it because it shows how people lived. Neat, I say, and tell her we should build our own cabin anyway. She sees how excited I am and says she will talk to Norm, but we should not count on it. I say I will work in the orchards to help pay.

"I know," Irma says, but she does not really know.

Catholics

Norm likes to say that he is good at talking to rich people. That is one of his specialties. Irma says it is better to talk to everyone the same way. She talks to me quietly about this until she is sure I understand. I say we do not know any rich people anyway.

"You never know," Irma says.

The richest kid I know lives five houses down, on the corner. His name is Gerald, and his family owns a carpet store in San Jose. We all say we are getting TVs, but Gerald already has one in his living room. He is two grades ahead of me and goes to Catholic school in corduroy pants and a white shirt. The rest of us go to Moorpark Elementary in our jeans and T-shirts.

During Easter vacation, Gerald and I ride bikes, and I want to be best friends. He takes me to a place I did not know about called the Rosicrucian Egyptian Museum. It is on the other side of San Carlos, which is one of the streets I am not allowed to cross. When we get there, Gerald leads me to a glass case where they have human heads the size of baseballs. He says they are shrunken heads from a lost civilization. They look like baby heads with their lips sewn shut. I wonder who would do that to a baby. I want to turn away, but I look because Gerald is watching me.

"Neat," I say, but I know he can tell that is not what I am thinking.

After we look at the heads, we sit outside and an ice cream truck comes with its music playing and Gerald buys me a popsicle. I ask him why the ice cream truck never comes to our neighborhood and he says because some of the houses are shitty. "Like yours," he says.

I am looking at Gerald, but I am thinking about that kid in the motel in Cheyenne. I push Gerald as hard as I can and he falls backward and I jump on him, but he rolls on top and pins me with his knees on my shoulders. I think he is going to drop spit down on my face, which is the worst thing kids do, but he shrugs and says he is sorry and wants to be friends again. I say okay, and he lets me up.

Gerald and I ride bikes all week, sometimes with other kids, but then we pedal away fast and lose them. Sometimes we let them catch up. Sometimes we just keep going. It is up to Gerald. On Good Friday, we ride to his school, St. Leo The Great School, and it has murals of God and a tower with a cross on top, like Mission Santa Clara. Gerald asks me if I believe in God and I say I do. Then he asks me what my favorite Holy Day is, and I figure he means holiday, so I say Christmas, because it has the longest vacation. He shakes his head and tells me Easter Sunday is holier than Christmas. It is his favorite because he gets up early and finds his Easter basket and then spends all morning eating candy in front of his TV and watching holy movies. He means the movies about Jesus all three of our stations run on Easter morning. He asks me if I want to come over and watch with him, and I do. But then he says no way, because I do not go to his school and I am not even a Catholic.

I tell Irma that Gerald is not my best friend anymore and she says maybe that is for the best because he is older. Norm tells me to call Gerald a Mackerel Snapper. Norm says Lutherans and Protestants are best. Then come some Catholics, but not Mexicans, if they are wetbacks or pachucos. Japs and chinks don't count, and Norm says we are lucky we don't have any kikes. Black people are at the bottom. *Jigaboos*, Norm calls them, or *coons*. He says *negro* is too polite. Norm and me are double lucky because we were born white.

"With white asses," Norm says.

That Easter Sunday, Irma takes me to the Congregational church near my school. It is the first time we go there, and Irma says she wants to walk because she used to walk all the time and it helps her think. She wants me to know that sometimes Norm is wrong about people. She says all people are the same, no matter what they believe or what color skin they have. Irma knows because she is a teacher and a Lutheran, and Lutherans always do the right thing, like being kind and fair and sticking up for people.

We do not walk home after church because Norm is waiting to pick us up.

Work-Ups

On summer nights we play work-ups in the street until it gets too dark to see the ball. Work-ups is for when you do not have enough players for teams. We play with two batters and just first base. Everybody else, except the pitcher and catcher and first baseman, is in the outfield, which is Bradley Avenue. As long as the batters get hits and work their way to first and back to home without getting out, they keep batting. If anyone catches a fly ball, they change places with that batter, but if you can hit like Gerald you can stay up forever. Gerald and I are the best players by a lot.

Margo, who lives next door to me, is pitching. I am the deepest kid in the field, but I am playing very shallow to make Gerald try to knock it over my head and pop up. Otherwise, it will be a long chase because we play with a hardball, and it will bounce and bounce and then just keep rolling. Gerald knows what I am doing because we both know his weakness, which is swinging too hard. Gerald tells Margo to lob an easy high one so he can really get a piece of it and she does and he smashes a line drive back into her face. The instant the ball hits her, we know it is bad. She does not scream, but blood spurts and she cups her hands over her nose and runs to her house.

None of us know what to do, so we sit on Margo's lawn and wait. I am next to Gerald and we pull up grass and then throw it back down. When he looks at me, I see he is crying and looks scared. We both know I had something to do with this, maybe caused it, even. Then he gets up and goes to Margo's front door and rings the bell and when Margo's mother opens it, he says he is sorry and that it was his fault but he did not mean to hurt her. I do not hear that, but it has to be what he says because Margo's mother nods and walks out on the lawn and we all stand up and she tells us Margo is going to be okay and we should all go home. I do not know if we all like Gerald better after that, but I know we like Margo better.

I tell Irma what happened, and she says Gerald did the right thing. Norm says Margo's dad should sue him.

Television

Norm is studying for his real estate license, but he leaves every morning with a lunch box Irma packs because he is still driving a Caterpillar tractor, like when he was working on Anderson Dam. Most days he stops at the 49er after work and sometimes Irma and I eat dinner before he gets home.

Irma gets a full-time teaching job at San Tomas Elementary, which sounds like a Catholic school but is just regular, except poorer. It is only three miles west of where we live, but there is almost nothing but orchards out there. Most of Irma's students come up from Mexico and live in camps, and she teaches them reading while their parents work the fruit and row crops. The men wear sombreros low over their eyes, and the women wear scarves over their faces. Norm calls them *frijole banditos* and laughs because he thinks his Mexican accent is funny. They are really called *braceros*, and Irma says they have a tough time because they only get to work for a couple months and then have to go back to Mexico. Most of them are gone by Christmas, when we get our first TV.

Norm likes "Friday Night Fights" on the *Gillette Cavalcade of Sports*, which he watches with his dinner on a TV tray. I like to watch

Crusader Rabbit, and *Adventure Time*, which shows serials like *Flash Gordon* and *Don Winslow of the Navy*, which I used to get to see on Saturday mornings at the Burbank Theater if Irma could find the extra nine cents it cost in her pocketbook. That did not happen very often, but it does not matter, because now we have a TV. I only have to wait until the next night to see what happens, like when Ming the Merciless is after Dale Arden, who is Flash Gordon's girlfriend. Don Winslow fights Nazis and Japs because he is in World War II. Norm calls them cliffhangers, as if I do not understand what that means.

I say I like *Crusader Rabbit* better anyway because it is a cartoon. Norm says cartoons are not funny enough for him. He says he wants to know why I like them, but I know he does not care. I say they help me think up adventures. He says I think too much, like it is a joke on me. I do not laugh, but what is funny is Norm is right. Since that bag of salt in the back seat between Salt Lake City and Reno.

Winchester

When Norm becomes a realtor, we move to a better house three blocks west. We are still in Burbank, but Irma says it is different because we are different. We have wall-to-wall carpeting, which Norm tells people is like walking on a bag of mice. He says Gerald's dad gave him a good deal on the carpeting because he wants Norm to sell his house for him so he can move to Los Gatos or Saratoga, where rich people are building mansions.

We are driving in Irma's Ford to pick her up at her school, and I tell Norm there are no mansions around except the Winchester Mystery House. He says he knows all about it. He says what I already know, that the widow of the guy who invented Winchester rifles built it for the ghosts of all the people the rifles killed. The mystery is why she kept adding rooms for thirty-eight years with no plan at all. Norm says that is what you get with a woman in charge.

I do not say anything.

Norm looks over at me from behind the wheel like he expects me to at least nod or something.

I stare straight ahead. I am thinking that Crazy Horse carried a Winchester.

Cadillac

Norm buys a used Cadillac with four doors and fins. It is old, but it is still a Cadillac, which he says is the kind of car he needs to drive his clients around. He says a realtor's car is his office and he needs a nice office. This makes us a two-car family like in the magazines Irma reads.

Sometimes Norm drives Irma and me to get hamburgers at Kirk's on the El Camino in Palo Alto. Norm says Kirk's has the best burgers because they are grilled over an open fire while you watch. We sit outside at picnic tables, like the ones at Seacliff, except instead of looking at the ocean we look at the El Camino. Irma always says there is more traffic than the last time. Norm says that is good for Kirk's business and Kirk is a friend of his and he is going to sell Kirk a new house. Norm is going to sell houses to all his friends because if you are friends with people, they owe you. Irma turns away like she wants to look at the traffic again.

One Friday night, Norm does not come home in time for his *Cavalcade of Sports*, and it gets later and later. This has happened plenty of times before, but I can tell this time is different. Irma tells me to get in the Ford. I ask where we are going, and she says she is not sure, but we drive to a new supermarket way out in Los Altos. It is open late, and I have never been in a store this big. We go up and down all the aisles, filling our cart with more groceries than we ever buy at one time.

When we get home, Norm is there and wants to know why Irma did not buy him his six-packs. Irma sends me to bed, but I hear her tell him it is her money and she will buy whatever she wants. That is all I remember until it is a lot later and I go into their bedroom to tell them to stop arguing. Irma is kneeling on the floor and Norm is standing over her. When they see me, they pretend nothing is wrong. I am nine years old. My half-sister is born when we live in that house.

Real Estate

We do not go anywhere on weekends because that is when Norm shows houses, but one Sunday we get dressed up and he drives us to South San Francisco in the Cadillac. Norm does not say why until we get there, and I get it that this is where Robin and Bonnie live now that they moved from Duluth, where they were friends with Norm and Irma and probably Bob too, but nobody mentions him.

Robin and Bonnie live on a steep hill, and all the houses are the same, except different colors. I think about how fast I could coast down their hill on my Phantom, but it is raining and they do not have any bikes. Bonnie says she is sorry there is nothing for me to do, but Norm says don't worry about it. Irma says I can read and pulls a book about the Pony Express out of her bag. So I have my new book, and Norm has his listings book and he and Robin sit in the living room and go through it. Irma and Bonnie take my baby sister into the kitchen to talk about how Bonnie is going to have a baby pretty soon. I listen to Norm tell Robin about each of the houses he has for sale, and how where we live is better than South San Francisco, where it rains all the time, like now. Robin says, "How about another highball?" and Norm sends me into the kitchen with their empty glasses to tell Bonnie they need refills.

IRMA

At the kitchen door, I hear Bonnie asking Irma if Norm really killed a man in Venezuela. It sounds like a joke, because Bonnie is giggling, but Irma wants to know where Bonnie heard that, and Bonnie says people in Duluth talked about it when Irma was in Texas. That is when they see me. Bonnie is holding my baby sister, so I hand Irma the highball glasses, and she says not to sneak up anymore. I say I did not hear anything, which Irma knows means I did.

Irma and Norm do not talk on the drive home, and I think about Venezuela. Irma is holding my sister on her lap, but she is reading my mind at the same time, and says Norm was very successful in Venezuela but he missed America and we are lucky he came back and is taking such good care of us. Norm reaches over and puts his hand on her knee.

Irma tucks me in that night, which surprises me because she stopped doing that when Norm started teasing me about being a baby. She sits on the bed and says she is proud of me and that Bob would be proud of me too. I ask her if she ever went up in Bob's fighter plane with him. She tips her head back and looks at the ceiling. When she looks back down at me she says no, not in a fighter because they have only one seat, but Bob used to take her up in one of the trainers and they would fly out over the Caribbean Sea. Once they flew out so far they could see Cuba. All the young pilots wanted to do that with their girlfriends.

Irma

Thursday is bowling night, so Irma and Norm go to Moonlight Lanes. They bowl on different teams with different bowling shirts and have drinks with all the other bowlers in all their different shirts. Norm does not drink beers anymore because realtors drink highballs. He brags to everyone about what a good bowler Irma is, even though she does not roll hard like he does.

Irma is what people call a natural athlete, and I get that from her. When she was a girl on that farm in Solon Springs, she could run faster than all the boys, and even high-jump over her head—which she did once at a track meet. I know because she showed me the ribbon. Her brother, Robby, was ten years older and a good baseball player. He could play every position but wanted to be a pitcher, so when he would practice on the farm Irma was his catcher. He would throw as hard as he could, and he had a curve-ball, but it did not matter because Irma could catch everything. So can I.

Norm

Norm picks me up after Little League practice. It is a Friday, and he is later than usual, but I am used to it. Norm always smokes when he drives, but this time when I climb into the front seat he's fumbling with the cigarette lighter and drops it on the floor and leaves it there. Pretty soon I am hanging out the passenger-side window and Norm is cutting very close to the bushes that grow high in some places along Moorpark. I think maybe he is doing it for me, and I reach out to touch some of the leaves as we pass. He is steering closer and closer and then swerving back, which is fun until we plow into the bushes. I bang my head hard on the dashboard. Norm looks over at me with a goofy face but does not say anything. That is when I see a policeman driving past the other way.

The policeman turns around and pulls up behind us. Norm tells me to keep quiet, and gets out. I watch through the back window. First Norm is talking a lot and the policeman is just looking at him. I think Norm is saying we are on our way to pick up Irma and my sister and go to Kirk's for burgers. But then Norm is nodding that he understands what the policeman is saying, then he holds his arms out like he is making a cross. I am sure we are not going to go to Kirk's because Norm is going to jail and I will have to go with him.

The policeman leads Norm over to my door and tells me I can hop out, which I do. The policeman sees my mitt and tells me I look like a ballplayer. He gives Norm a disgusted look and then says he is going to drive us home. Norm looks relieved, even though the policeman tells him to sit in the back of the police car like he is under arrest and I will be riding in front.

When we get to the corner before our house, Norm asks the policeman if we can walk the last block.

"The neighbors," Norm says.

The policeman pulls over and turns to me. It is like he is going to tell me something important but then changes his mind. I wait, and he finally asks if I play Little League.

"I didn't make Little League," I lie, without even thinking about it.

The policeman looks at Norm, and then back at me like he wants to know why.

"I'm not good enough."

We get out of the police car, and I do not look at Norm, but he puts his hand on my shoulder. As we walk home, he tells me Irma does not have to know everything about what happened, about the Cadillac breaking down.

When we get to our house, Irma's Ford is in the driveway. Norm stops us, bends down, and says he knows he can count on me, that I will be a good man. I memorize his face, naked with cowardice.

Listings

Norm sells his first exclusive listing, which is a big deal because now he will get more listings, and he and Irma go out to celebrate. I fall asleep watching TV. When I wake up it is early morning and I am still on the floor and a snowy test pattern is on the screen. I do not know why Irma and Norm left me there, but figure they are still asleep because their door is closed. I go out and look at the Cadillac and there is throw-up all over the outside of the passenger door. I clean it off with my arm. *The neighbors.*

Patch Avenue

When I am twelve we move again, two more blocks west to Patch Ave, and we are different there too, like we are every time we move. Irma still has her Ford convertible, but it is going to be mine soon enough. One house down is my new best friend, who is good at every sport. He and I are the best athletes in our grade, and by freshman year everybody knows who we are. His parents are friends with Irma and Norm, which we like at first, but then his dad starts saying how he and Irma should be together. He is just being funny, but we do not like it. We never say anything to each other about it, and that makes us better friends.

Campbell

The summer before my sophomore year, we move to our last house with Norm. It is in Campbell, which is next to Burbank, and I still go to the same school. It is better to be from Campbell, so now that is where Norm says we are from.

Our new house is a two-story with a bedroom upstairs for me. Irma says we are going to stay in this house for a long time. She buys furniture and rugs for the living room and puts my little bench next to the fireplace to remind us of when I was little, which she says makes her happy. She has a better teaching job now, so we have more money. Norm is still talking about the big sales he's got going, but most afternoons I see his Cadillac parked at the 49er.

One day, when we have been in the new house for not even a couple months, Irma picks me up from school after sports, and when we get home there is one of Norm's *For Sale* signs in the front yard. Irma pulls it up and takes it inside. When Norm comes home and sees his *For Sale* sign in the living room, he yells for us to get in there and then tells Irma he is selling the house because he can make a little money on it and it is his house to sell if he wants because they are married.

Irma says we will see about that, and Norm slaps her so hard she falls. I know what I am going to do, and time speeds up. I go to the fireplace and pick up my bench. I am going to kill Norm with my little bench. I wind up like I'm going to throw a pitch and hit him in the side of his head without letting go.

Norm staggers, then whirls, swinging, and hits me in the face with his fist. It hurts, but I do not go down. I am mostly surprised. Norm is surprised too. I am still holding my bench, like I might hit him again. He is starting to bleed, then blood is gushing down the side of his head. He touches the gash and then looks at his hand. When he looks up, we lock eyes.

He looks away, snarling at Irma, and then leaves fast, like he knows everything is different now. The last thing he says as he slams out the front door is that we are going to find out how tough I really am.

That is what I want to know too.

Walk Like a Man

Irma starts seeing men. I play three sports, and she comes to my games, but we are not the same. We only talk about Norm once, when she tells me she got a restraining order and is getting a divorce. I'm proud of her, but I do not say that. I am thinking about Venezuela, which is really thinking about when I am going to see Norm again and how we are going to find out how tough I am.

By my junior year, everybody knows me because of football. Irma has had a couple of boyfriends, which is hard on my sister because Norm is still her father. She is in third grade and never gets in trouble but is sad all the time. I can tell she does not like any of Irma's boyfriends, but what can she do? With me, they want to be pals and talk football. I gain more than three thousand yards of total offense that year, which is a big deal to them, as if they played, which I doubt. Sometimes this embarrasses Irma because we can both tell they are kind of afraid of me.

Everybody cool at my school smokes, especially the popular girls, and if you are really cool you drink too. I do not smoke, but I drink all the time. Irma knows, but the only thing she ever says to me about drinking is that it is expensive. She does not know we break into houses to steal our booze.

My life becomes a frictionless slide toward graduation. Nothing is at stake. I do not have a girlfriend—I work a black market of emotionless transactions: one girl for Homecoming, another for the back seat of Irma's old Ford, another for just riding around drinking beers and talking. My grades do not matter because of football, which comes naturally. I never even think about it. I am uncanny. The newspapers say I am hard to bring down. I get good grades anyway.

My friends are the guys I play sports with. The usual horrors of high school mean nothing to us. There is a popular song called "Walk Like a Man" that we mock because the group is from New Jersey and the front man, Frankie Valli, sings in falsetto, but it is in all our heads: "No woman's worth crawlin' on the earth . . ." That is all we need to know.

When a new girl named Clydia shows up, she is immediately the cutest girl in school, like she is Natalie Wood. But she tells the first girl she tries to be friends with that she lives in a foster home, and word gets around. She seems shy and tough, and I want to get to know her, but I do not even say hi. Then a pock-faced guy on the football team has a date with her or maybe just gives her a ride home but comes to school the next morning sniffing his middle finger for everyone to see. I do not say anything. All the guys laugh, and I am surprised that so many girls are giggling. I do not laugh, but I do not stick up for her either.

A year behind me there is this soft, friendless kid named Wayne who everybody somehow knows gave a blow job to a bum behind the Moonlight Lanes. Some of my teammates make blowing sounds when he walks past in the halls, and those same girls giggle. One day during lunch period some seniors tackle him and pants him on the lawn where half the school is eating lunch. I feel sorry for him, but I do not help him. It is like with Clydia. I think about being a coward, still hearing Frankie Valli in my head. I wonder about the men Irma is seeing.

Prom

My French teacher, Miss Darnay, is a chaperone at the senior prom. I come late without a date to show how cool I am. Miss Darnay stops me at the door and says she wants to talk to me, so we walk around a corner of the gym. She says my arrogance is unattractive and is getting in my own way, especially in her French I class, which I am taking as a goof with mostly freshman girls, and now also tonight, when she can tell that all I am about is making some of my classmates feel uncool, inferior. Is that what I want? Make people feel inferior? She says my whole attitude is wrong and it will be a big problem if I take it with me to college.

"And you can be so charming," she says, with a kind of smirk, and I see she has some attitude going there herself.

Miss Darnay is slender and in her low heels as tall as me. This is her first year out of Chico State, and she is twenty-three. I reach in my pocket for the half pint of Jose Cuervo I have been sipping and hold it out to her. She cocks her head as if I am way out of line, which I get that I am.

"Who do you think you are?" she smirks. "James Dean?"

I tell her I do not know who James Dean is, which she has to know is a lie. We stand there with me holding out the Cuervo and her starting to smile.

"You like this James Dean guy?"

She takes my bottle and puts it in the side pocket of the navy blazer she always wears. "You go to your prom," she says. "We'll talk about this another time."

Someone sees this, and it gets around that I have something going on with Miss Darnay. I say nothing.

Venezuela

Uncle Jack and Pops come to California for my high school graduation. The next day I take them to the beach, which they call the Pacific Ocean and have never seen. I drive them in the old Ford to the same Seacliff State Beach where Norm took Irma and me with Adolph. I do not know why I take them there. Maybe because it is where I first saw the ocean, or maybe it is the only beach I know with picnic tables.

It is a warm June day, not cold and rainy like when we came with Adolph. We sit at one of those same tables with the carved initials, and eat sandwiches Irma made. All around us are families in bathing suits, grilling chorizo and playing transistor radios. Jack and Pops are both wearing the suits they wore to my graduation. They are going back to Duluth in the morning.

"Pretty nice here," Jack says.

"But crowded," says Pops.

"We're three generations," Jack says, like he is opening a meeting. We talk a little about Bob. Pops says Bob liked spaghetti and could play the piano by ear. Jack says Bob was his hero. Somewhere in my head, I am still a little kid, thinking maybe I will ask how Bob died, but Irma and I talked about it and that is enough. So I put that away and ask Jack about being shot down and he tells me he was saved by the French Resistance. Pops shakes his head and says Jack was MIA for six weeks. All that time he thought Jack was dead, Bob was alive, and then when Bob was dead, Jack was alive.

I wonder why I did not know any of that.

Jack says he and Norm were friends when they were young, and after Norm split with Irma, he would call Jack in the middle of the night and talk about all the real estate deals he had going.

"He also talked about you," Jack says. "All about your football."

"He killed a guy in Venezuela," I blurt. "Right?"

Jack and Pops give each other looks like they both want the other to take over. Finally, Jack runs his hands through his hair and says the story is that Norm ran over a Venezuelan guy when he was driving his Caterpillar on the job, or maybe it was not on the job and Norm was in his car, but either way, Norm got out of it because he was working for Standard Oil.

"Was he drunk?"

This surprises them, makes them uneasy. Maybe I am not what they expected. What the fuck, I think, neither of them has seen me since I was a little boy.

Pops says he never liked Norm and everything about Norm makes him mad. He says Irma made a mistake being with Norm, which makes me mad. Pops is right, but that does not help Irma. I cannot tell what Jack is thinking when he goes on about how Irma was just a farm girl who knew how to milk cows but went to college and met Bob and decided to be a teacher. Bob was so crazy about her he would get jealous. I do not like any of that, and I guess Jack can tell, because he fake-punches me in the arm and says Bob would be proud of me.

We all look at one another. Finally, Pops says he heard Adolph is dead.

The 49er

I get a scholarship to play football at Cal, and that summer I work construction to get stronger and make extra money. After we get paid one Friday, the guys on my crew decide to go to the 49er. Fuck it, I think, it's probably time. I do not see Norm when we walk in. We go to the back to play shuffleboard. When I look around again, there is Norm, sitting at the front corner of the bar like the regular he is. I must have walked right past him. I have not seen him since I hit him with my little-kid bench. He is heavier, not so skinny anymore, older. He looks like Adolph.

I turn away and take my turn at the shuffleboard. When I look back at Norm, he nods at me and I see him signaling to the bartender to send us a round of beers. The guys welcome the beers and ask me who the old drunk is.

I walk up to the bar, and Norm gets off his stool, looking a little shaky. He holds out his hand and says he heard I got a full ride at Cal. He does not say anything about Irma. I am thinking I know everything about him and he knows nothing about me. I watch his face as he registers what is coming. It is the face I memorized that day the policeman drove us home, the face telling me to act like a man—*naked with cowardice*.

IRMA

I slap him hard and wait for him to recover, to make eye contact, and then slap him again, harder, and he falls back against the bar.

"Hey, hey, hey, kid!" the bartender shouts.

"It's okay," Norm says. "He's my son."

Part II

...

RIVER JETTY

1

(RASCAL)

That little boy, that kid, forms himself by what he forgets as much as by what he remembers. The past would always be there, but to remember everything is madness. Better to sort the scraps of his memory—snapshots, really, of the long strangeness of his life opening like a TV show he would write later:

> *Single-engine Cessna banks a turn, comes in low . . .*

Umbilical

A son hating his stepfather, searching for the character of his true father, is an old story. The center of the story, though, is not one of the fathers or even the son. It is the mother, Irma, and it starts with her telling her son that he is a good little boy, looking into his eyes and saying it will be easy for him to be kind and fair because that is his instinct, his nature beneath all else. He will always do the right thing. Did he understand?

He would worry that question over and over—sometimes before sleep, or on a summer day looking up at the sky, on his back on a lawn he has just mowed for a quarter. Above the clouds he follows the contrails of a jet streaking white across the infinite blue. Maybe that one is his favorite, an F-86 Sabre jet, but will it ever be *his* Sabre jet? The size of his future bothers him. He will try to be good, but it will be hard.

Nothing is precise in his head, none of the little pieces fit together, but he can see Irma clearly. In a very strange way he can see himself too, from a distance that surprises him. Irma is smiling, with a bright scarf around her neck. He is his mother's son.

POV

Let me tell you about him.

He looked like Irma, with all her blondeness, and there was the same recklessness in his light eyes. Something they shared but would never talk about. Irma saw this, and it worried her, but he had to learn for himself. When he tore open his arm falling out of a cherry tree, she made him look at it. She told him it was hard to look at but if he did not look directly at it he would not remember what he needed to remember, not learn what he needed to learn. The gash was deep and long, from hooking the inside of his elbow on a dead branch as he fell. They were in an emergency room. He was seven.

After that he was never afraid to look but thought of it as being tough, not the knowledge Irma intended for him. So he missed things. Courage was important, and he had been a brave little boy, but as a teenager courage was harder to prove. Cockiness was not the same thing, and he was struggling to define himself, although he did not think that way yet.

When he found out Norm had had a woman on the side, he was not surprised. He did not know what to do, but could not let it go. She was a secretary at a rival real estate office. Not beautiful like

Irma, but cute. Cute. Norm was still seeing her. He thought about fucking her cuteness just to let Norm know. That is what Norm would have done, and he felt like he might have that power. Maybe he did.

It was confusing.

Irma was more cheerful than he could remember, telling neighbors she had turned the page. Her life was flowering again. She hung a Currier & Ives print of sleighing in New England in the small dining room and had other teachers over for dinner. When he left for Berkeley, she walked him to her old Ford, now his, and told him not to worry about her *anymore*. That seemed a funny word to him, and it might have resonated if he had not been so struck by how pretty Irma was and how strong she seemed.

Irma smiled. She must have known there would be changes between them, even changes in the way they perceived each other, and that would be fine. In the end neither of them wanted to be trapped in a life they did not choose if they ever chose at all. That was their solidarity, and she was not done with him.

Drift

After a year of football at Cal, he walked away from his scholarship and got late admission into San Jose State by letting the athletic director think he would play there when he got his eligibility back. Never going to happen.

Irma did not ask about his plans. "I thought you liked football" is all she said, letting whatever she was thinking trail into a look he did not recognize. They were in her kitchen. He had stopped by to tell her he had left Cal. He studied her face, wondering what she saw in his. He had hated not being the best guy on the field, or maybe he was just afraid, not tough enough to play big-time football. Did Irma see that? She turned to pour herself more coffee. She had never pushed him. She turned back. He waited. Irma shrugged. He was never going to forget that shrug.

San Jose State killed time, even though he mostly filled his days without going to class. It did not occur to him that education could lead to something, like a job he might like. He had never known anyone who liked their job, except maybe Irma. He had never thought about things adding up, or the cumulative effect of small mistakes. He reconnected with high school friends who went to

City College or had flunked out or gotten pregnant and married or had abortions or just gotten jobs. It all seemed normal enough, but there was an unfamiliar blankness in his life. He let his hair grow and began to drift, mostly getting stoned instead of drunk. Sometimes both. He did not care. He was feckless, a word he had not yet read.

Everything had always worked out, like now, when Bob's GI Bill benefits covered his college tuition plus $91 a month so he did not need a scholarship. That was a big part of knowing he had it made, which made him ashamed and faintly proud at the same time, so he forgot about it. Not that he actually forgot. He just did not think about it.

One of Irma's boyfriends was high enough in the local National Guard to get some of his friends in so they did not have to worry about the draft. Irma helped with that even though he was a "sole surviving son of a deceased veteran," which meant he had Bob's classification, 4-A. He would not be sent to Vietnam until World War II vets were called up. He did have it made.

That Christmas Eve, he stopped by Irma's house for a drink on his way to a party with friends from high school. She was having some people over, and, surprising to him, he did not know any of them. Some were close to his age, like the two first-year teachers Irma now had renting his old upstairs bedroom. They were both attractive, and flirtatious with the young men they had invited to the party. Listening to the four of them talk about their grown-up lives made him uncomfortable, but he hung around them and stayed later than he had planned.

When he was leaving, Irma followed him out on her front porch.

She was not worried, she said, but maybe he should remember how expensive drinking was.

"How many drinks did I have?" he said, suddenly defensive.

"I don't count drinks," Irma said.

"Two," he said.

"Four."

He had to get out of there, not just off Irma's porch. He had never felt the fear of not making it and what that might mean. A cold winter fog had come up. Irma shivered. Now what? He leaned in for Irma's goodbye kiss on his cheek.

"You'll figure it out," she whispered.

Cadillac Plastics

Irma called him on New Year's Day and asked him how he liked San Jose State. This threw him until she said she was thinking about going back to school. She would earn more as a teacher with every additional education credit. She told him it was an obvious thing to do. Sometimes you think something is enough for you, but then maybe not. You have to decide that, and she had.

"But I don't have much choice about where," she went on. "Stanford doesn't have any of the right classes, and everywhere else is too far away. What do you think?"

"You're not really asking me," he said.

"I read it's a 'party school.'"

He took stock. Irma was right, San Jose State had an embarrassing reputation, but he had met some people he liked. Through a girl from Beverly Hills who was bitter about not getting into Smith, he hit it off with a guy going to Stanford, who was always mocking it as "The Harvard of the West." He did not know what it meant not to get into Smith, and all he knew about Stanford was that the football coach had not recruited him. He did not know anything about Harvard or anyone who went there or even anyone who talked about how important it was. He did not know any of that, but he was interested.

His new friend, Rawls, was from Malibu, and was heading back south to finish school at the new University of California at Irvine. He should come. They could get a place on the beach. Go in the water every day. The Wedge. When he asked Irma what she thought, she told him he was not really asking, and just like that, he transferred, arriving as an English major but switching immediately to art. He loved sitting in darkened rooms looking at slides of paintings. The glamorous abstract expressionists predictably became his favorite painters, although he was drawn to Joseph Cornell, whose shallow wooden boxes of shooting-gallery birds, distressed reproductions of Renaissance portraits, and perhaps a humble cork, held odd resonance for him.

He called Irma from a pay phone in the Sandpiper Lounge in Laguna to tell her he was going to Mexico for spring break and mentioned that he had switched his major to art. He was learning a lot. Maybe he would become an artist, a painter of ideas even. Irma told him she did not know he could draw, and that his Uncle Jack could *really* draw and had wanted to be a cartoonist, but went to work for Armour Star meats instead. He had never heard that about Jack. Before they hung up, Irma encouraged him by saying Jack probably would have been happier as a cartoonist than selling ham.

He did not tell Irma that the studio classes were hilariously loose and undemanding. He especially appreciated not having to draw a white bowl of hard-boiled eggs to get a good grade in drawing. He was a grateful fraud until it sunk in that art was about ideas, not craft. This excited him. Art stars like Frank Stella and his wife, the young critic Barbara Rose, were in residence. David Hockney passed through with great style that included polka-dot suits.

He began to get ideas about how he might fit into that world. Many of his teachers were close to his age, a gang of emerging minimalists. The slick, seductive surfaces of their pieces echoed hot rods and surfboards. Everyone used the word *conceptual*. He learned to talk about *conceptualism's systems of meaning*.

He was the best writer among the student artists, and, showing off, he used language in his pieces. He blew up a snapshot of Irma and Bob until they were ghosted and wrote *Photography Is About Time* across the pointilization. Speaking as a critic of his own work, he said, "You can point a camera at only one thing at a time." Instructors noticed and became friendly. He sent away for a heat gun and shopped at Cadillac Plastics in Anaheim for Plexiglas and polyester resin—plastics with memory. He made lopsided boxes with different-colored sides and then put his gun on them. It made no difference that he could not draw.

Shedding Skin

He felt his independence in a new way, maybe *launched* was the word, with his life finally opening beyond his adolescence. Irma had simply released him, although he did not think about it that way. She remained vivid in his mind, but he seldom called. They were both busy, anyway. Him with his new ideas and Irma with whatever . . . His sister, probably, but he did not think about her either.

He lived on the ocean, just south of the river jetty. On weekends, he stayed up all night with a woman down the beach, drinking and smoking and finally falling into bed as the sun was coming up. It did not occur to him that she would get pregnant. She was a little older, in her first year teaching at a grammar school in Fountain Valley. She said she wanted an abortion but did not want to go through it with him. This surprised him. When he told her it was not right for her to have to go through it alone, she told him he could help pay—but to stay away.

His roommate, Rawls, arranged it in Santa Monica, drove her there and picked her up. Rawls told him he had gone through the same thing with the girl who did not get into Smith. For Rawls, it was an exercise in competence, like settling an old debt. For him, it was a relief. He did not know about the girl who did not get into Smith, but for the girl down the beach, his girl, it took a kind of courage he did not know about.

When he called her that night, she said she was done with him, like she was *shedding skin*. Her words. He was grateful and ashamed, but also confused. Was she dumping him? That never happened. Was he letting her go? She was a terrific girl, curious and so smart, with a master's in primary education from a good Midwestern university. Lovely too, with easy curves and fine, tanned skin. And it meant something to him that she was a teacher, like Irma.

On one of their first beach walks he had cracked her up, telling her she was lucky she had a job that did not depend on the weather. After she laughed, she tilted her head and smiled at him as if amused by a precocious child. He told her about Irma taking him to a PTA meeting before he was old enough to go to school. She was to be introduced as a new substitute teacher and she could not afford a babysitter. He was afraid the parents would not like her because she brought her kid along. He listened as hard as he could to what they said. Even as a little boy, he could listen. They said they were glad to have a new teacher and joked that she was lucky to have a job that did not depend on the weather—like construction, or fruit and row crops. It was strange to him how details of his childhood would come back to him like that, but there they were.

That *shedding of skin* remained locked away until years later, when he was sitting in a café near Gare du Sud in Paris, reading the *International Herald Tribune*, and there was his old roommate's name at the top of a piece about a $1,000,000 hash bust by Royal Canadian Mounted Police. Rawls had been arrested in North Vancouver with a van packed with bricks of hash under the floor. Authorities said the van had been customized for that purpose. What he remembered about the girl was how she reminded him of Irma, and not just because she was a teacher. She had simply decided she did not want what she was getting and went for something else— like Irma driving to California. Or maybe she moved back home to Wisconsin and married the guy who had always been in love with her and helped him through medical school. And then maybe she turned around again and was waiting for Rawls at some safe house in North Vancouver.

He turned that over. His brain felt crammed, but nothing of his time with her was precise. What did they do those nights? It was fuzzy. What was her music? What did she drink? He could not tell himself their story with any detail, not even her name. The abortion was all he remembered, and he was not even there.

Then an image, running with her across the sand at night, naked, into the dark surf.

Kathleen.

Chemeketa Park

After college he found a small cabin in the Santa Cruz Mountains and worked construction part-time. He thought about how he might become an artist, but his reality was shoveling asphalt on new school playgrounds in new subdivisions, paving the orchards he had played in as a kid. He called Irma sometimes to tell her where he had been working or he might drop in on a Sunday and make himself a sandwich. Irma would always ask what he was reading and he always had a book to talk about but never with much enthusiasm.

She started giving him books, like when he was little. Some by writers he had not thought to read—*In Cold Blood* by Truman Capote, and *The Hero with a Thousand Faces* by the mythologist Joseph Campbell, and there were many more. Irma liked writers of her generation, especially Steinbeck. "Girls in Their Summer Dresses" by Irwin Shaw was her favorite story. She also liked *Gone with the Wind*, but told him he did not have to bother. He read it anyway, which pleased her.

His cabin was in Chemeketa Park, a summer-home community founded deep in the redwoods in the 1920s for escape from the heat of the Valley, where Irma lived. It was close to where his Cub Scout friend's father built their family cabin. The one time he drove over to see it, the cabin looked tired and empty, like nobody used it anymore. He did not think anything about that, remembering instead what he had been told about the redwoods being from before anyone came to America and how Irma had explained how wrong that was.

He liked that Chemeketa was Kalapuya for "old camping ground." The streets had tribe names like Comanche Trail. He lived on Oglala Warpath, and how cool was that? He remembered his favorite Indian book. Crazy Horse was Oglala.

Irma told him if he liked the cabin so much he should buy it, even though she had to know he did not have the money. "Something to think about," Irma said. She had some friends, a couple from Michigan, who had bought a small resort on Swan Lake near Bigfork, Montana. It was a collection of five cabins, a dock, and a lodge from the 1940s. The couple figured they could retire there with some income, or maybe sell the cabins to friends like Irma and make it the kind of summer club they had grown up with in the Midwest. Irma was interested in this, but she also thought Montana real estate would never appreciate more than what she could afford in the booming Santa Clara Valley. When she explained this to him he knew that *something to think about* meant he should not hate real estate because of Norm.

Well, fuck Norm, and he would love to buy his cabin. Successful musicians and dope dealers prized the old summer houses and acted like hipster country gentlemen when they lucked into buying one. They drove Porsches, dressed up in paisley scarfs, and bought art. He envied them. These were not guys who blew through their money with girlfriends they turned into coke whores. The dealers he knew were interesting, entrepreneurial. He thought about that too.

He also knew people who danced with their dogs and tried to get their cats high, mountain hippies who wanted to get to know their animals—a self-satisfied life view as banal as a macaw taught to say, "Far Out!" People who did drugs were *heads*. All hippies were heads by definition, but not all heads were hippies. He was a head. He liked the hippie women, though, with their long silky hair like Mama Michelle, and they liked him back. They got stoned in the redwoods or at the beach or went to bars and explained themselves to each other.

There was one time at a dive bar in Los Gatos with a girl he had known in passing at Berkeley who had recently joined a local commune when he said he had a Hamlet complex. Like the confused prince, he was in the process of figuring himself out as he despaired over his mother's bad marriage. He did not mention Irma by name. The girl was sympathetic and wanted to know more.

He sighed and said he was diagnosed at Cal, where he had been recruited not for football but for a program that studied creatively screwed-up students with exceptionally high IQs. It was like Ken Kesey volunteering to take LSD for the PhD psych candidates at Stanford. He implied he sometimes had flashbacks to his unhappiness as a little boy. It was a dirty string of one lie leading to another. He conveniently forgot he had come up with his bullshit Hamlet complex when he, himself, was high on acid.

"You must really hate her," the girl said, and went home with him to his cabin.

IRMA

In the morning she was gone and he never saw her again but he remembered everything he had said to her about Irma. It made him sick with betrayal. He was not sure when it would catch up with him, but it would always be coming, and even if Irma would never know about any of this, it made him more anxious to make it up to her.

He started working construction full time and saving money. Maybe he could buy his cabin, but there was something very flat in having that as his goal. Then, one morning, on a job in Cupertino, he saw a bus of *braceros* with their lowered hats, looking straight ahead like they always did. He thought about all the children Irma had taught to read English at San Tomas. He remembered sitting with her on the backyard step in Burbank, sounding out words so fast he would make her laugh.

After work that day, instead of drinking beers with his crew, he started to read again, like in grammar school, when every new book filled him with impatience for the next, a hunger he had lost in college. He read sitting on tractors at lunch and during work breaks and every night on his porch in the redwoods. He read in Joseph Campbell that if you do that—read and read and read—the right books can give you "a nice, mild, slow-burning rapture all the time." That was fine and he liked the idea more than he liked Campbell, but for him it was more like a series of small explosions lighting him up with ideas that, misleadingly or not, made him feel smarter. He knew he had a solid education, but now he saw new levels. Most important, though, and beneath it all, he was reading to make Irma proud of him again.

California

Irma never talked politics.

"I'm past all that," she would say, and she was, except for school funding. He assumed she was against the war, although he knew she had voted for Ronald Reagan for governor, and it was Reagan who had called out the National Guard in Berkeley. They never argued over any of that, but she told him he would remember some things about his life differently when he was older. She would smile sometimes and say that little things could mean a little too much.

He must have appeared naive to her, but she listened to him seemingly without judgment.

He had a number of ways he talked about the '60s, but they were not important except as evidence that he was polluted by trends. By saying he believed in nothing, he believed in everything. Or so he said. His experiences were predictable, more ordinary than he thought at the time. He had joined SDS, gone to class on acid, written embarrassing poetry. He had met Timothy Leary, who was wrong about everything. The higher you got, the *less* you knew, not the other way around. It was obvious, but that did not stop him.

The drugs were always kicking in. "One Toke Over the

Line" . . . yes, yes, endlessly ironic. He was from California in a way he had not considered before. It was fine that the songs said California had the best waves and the best girls and the best dope, but the day after "sex, drugs, and rock and roll" was what he stupidly said to an Oakland Police sergeant to explain what he thought was so fucking funny about martial law in Berkeley, all he could actually call to mind was how beautiful tear gas looked floating down Telegraph Avenue in the evening light.

He saw beauty everywhere. It filled his brain without thinking. Sometimes he would ride around smoking weed and wonder at the towering eucalyptus separating the orchards or the live oak overhanging the tiny roads winding into the mountains. He was vain about the landscape, as if the trees were his because he could name them.

He was proud too, of the revolution, such as it was, but like his friends, like everyone he knew, really, he was provincial in ways he did not recognize until he went east and saw how America actually worked—what power was and what you had to do to get it in an established order built on generations of wealth.

When he was ten, Irma had told him Bob probably would have gone into the airline business. Bob and a friend, another pilot, had talked about starting small as soon as the war was over and eventually challenging Eastern Airlines for their routes between New York and Florida. He did not understand what she was telling him. He did not remember Florida except what Irma had told him about how much fun they had when he was little and they went to Palmetto Beach near Pensacola. He did not like not remembering, and not understanding bothered him more.

Irma saw this in his face and told him again how they had everything they could ever want here in California. He nodded that he understood but then blurted out that he did not want any other lives. She took him by the hand and sat him down on the cinderblock step to the backyard and together they went over the sunny weather and the orchards and the new roads and the new schools. Irma said Bob would have liked California too, he would have loved the trees.

Beirut

Bob went down at twenty-five, Irma was twenty-five when he was born, and that was the birthday he was about to celebrate—a dangerous, stupid age to be broke and think you are gifted with no evidence of that being true. He had applied to the MFA program at Irvine and not gotten in. He was belligerent. He kept compartments of ambitions in his mind like Cornell boxes. He had never even flown on Eastern Airlines. Was he an artist yet? All he knew, all he trusted, was that he could remake himself with corny showmanship.

He went to the beach and squeezed lemon juice on his hair.

Being from California, he also believed that everything started there. Vietnam was a California war, his war, even if he was never in it. A lot of guys lied about that, saying they could not talk about it because, man, had they seen some heavy shit. They had taken out so many Japs and Nazis as little boys that their imaginations twisted into guilt. So yeah, they lied. He did not lie, but thought he might have been an okay marine.

Maybe he should have gone. Just signed up. Before he was five, Pops had taught him how to salute, and schooled him in the family history. The Clan McDonell of Glengarry overrun on the left flank and riddled with grapeshot at bloody Culloden, 1746. Paying the price of refusing to give up the kilt and tartan. Flight from the Highlands, chased across Ireland, storm-tossed, courageous passage to the New World. Indian fighters on the wild frontier, years of settlement skirmishes, Micmac (Nova Scotia), Ojibwa (Minnesota), 1820–1850. Allen McDonell, superb rifleman and sniper, 1st Minnesota Volunteer Infantry, Bull Run, Antietam, Fredericksburg, Gettysburg, killed hand-to-hand, age twenty-two at Pickett's Charge, 1863. Meinrad "Pops" McDonell (himself), Company M, 341st Infantry, 1st Machine Gun Battalion, mowing down Krauts at Belleau Wood, 1917–1918. John Charles "Jack" McDonell, 8th Air Force Bomber Command, sixty-seven daylight, precision, and strategic bombing runs over occupied Europe out of High Wycombe, England, 1942–1945. Bob.

When he watched the war on television, he wanted the romantic correspondent life with all its glamorizing of the ambivalent moral issues of the war. Not the war itself. So he had demonstrated against it. Now what? He was not so much stalled as becalmed, letting his days go by. He became desperate. What if he took his cameras and 4-A deferment and went east, first to Europe, then across Asia to Vietnam? Become some kind of journalist? Not so much turning his back on the war as slipping in the back way. He would transform himself again.

He drove from the beach to Irma's with his mind churning. It was a hot Sunday in July. He had been gone from her house since he was seventeen. She had let him go so easily he had hardly noticed until now, sitting at the picnic table in her backyard. She brought out a Mexican beer for him and a glass of Chablis for herself. When he told her his plan, her eyes tightened. In that moment he understood that his war was not her war, and he could never know what she had felt, or was feeling now about the turns in her life—the loss. This spooked him. He realized he was there for her permission.

"I have to get out of here," he said.

"Do you need any money?"

With $1,000 from Irma, he bought an H-16 Bolex and a one-way ticket to Amsterdam. Two months later, he was sitting on a rooftop in Tehran, listening to the draft lottery on Armed Forces Radio with a dozen Peace Corps volunteers—most of them hiding out from the draft that none of his high school friends had to worry about, thanks to Irma's National Guard now-ex-boyfriend.

It was sweltering, and they had a tub of beers. Anyone with a high number was not going to get called up, so there was nothing to wait out, and a couple guys with high numbers announced that they were resigning the Peace Corps the next day. They did not need the deferment anymore. Why wait? More important to him was why he had waited, like some kind of loser, to get out into the world.

He had even borrowed money from Irma, which shamed him now. And he had not been in touch with her since he had let himself out of her backyard through the side gate with her check. Irma never said anyone was full of shit, but he knew she thought that when she said someone was full of bologna. It was silly. He teased her about it. Now what?

The next morning he flew to Beirut, landing in the middle of what became Black September when King Hussein of Jordan enforced a bloody military rule to put down an insurrection by the Palestine

Liberation Organization (PLO). Most of the journalists lived in the Phoenicia Hotel and hired cars every day to take them to the civil war in Amman—usually getting back to the hotel in time for a few drinks with Air France stewardesses. He could not afford to stay at the Phoenicia, but he went to the war and sometimes to the bar, where he met an Air France stewardess from Nantes. Her name was Nadine, and she wore her bright blond hair chopped short, almost boyish, against the long, ironed style of women her age. He tried to concentrate.

Nadine was flirtatious but usually unsympathetic to all the low-level expat journalists like him sitting around hotel bars telling each other ironic stories about other journalists faking it—operating without credentials, fudging datelines, but knowing that everyone faked it sometimes. He was faking it—no real assignments, not really making any money, even though he had looked at those hijacked airliners on the ground, and walked the PLO camp in Karameh looking for sources. Or had he just been playing a part? Vaudeville, maybe.

At least he had met Nadine.

Nadine was *random*, his new favorite word, and he wanted *random*, maybe just not as *random* as driving around the Jordan Valley trying to nail down whatever solidarity there was between the Palestinians and the IRA, which was his favorite rumor. Now, *that* was *conceptual*, and it could be his art, like in college, his own media practice, although he did not talk like that to Nadine. He was curating himself into a collection of experiences, and Nadine would be one of them. Much easier than journalism. She found him interesting anyway, some kind of cultural mongrel.

Nadine flew Paris-Beirut-Rome-Paris once a week. In Beirut, she bought gold jewelry that she wore to Rome, where she sold it. She explained this to him after he told her how important it was to document the rise of Al Fatah, the PLO faction controlled by Yasser Arafat. She smiled, ruffled her hair with both hands, and invited him to Rome. A couple of wire machines clattered in a corner of the bar.

Staying alone in a hostel in Venice after Nadine told him she had a fiancé in Paris, he heard two art history grad students talking about him through the thin wall. They were the tall Swedish women with perfect English he had been drinking with at the café next door. Standing at the zinc bar, he told them about Syrian tanks joining the PLO in the streets of Amman. How brave to be there, they told him. What they were saying now, in the next room, was that if he was who he said he was he would not be staying in their shitty hostel.

This knocked him back more than losing Nadine. He felt humiliated, totally busted, and the search for the best hotel for who he said he was would become another subtext of his life. He hoped so, anyway. Listening through the wall in that moment, he ached to be successful, self-aware, not full of shit, and then, suddenly, not full of bologna. There was a storm of ambition inside his head, but he had no next steps, except to quit fucking around. He remembered Irma telling him she thought he liked football. He thought about the river jetty. He wondered about those Eastern Airlines routes between New York and Florida.

He started to dream about going down—not nightmares exactly, but with his plane falling from the sky the way they never do except in cartoons, at a perfect ninety-degree angle. He would be in first class, looking around, and everyone would be strapped in but no one would be screaming or even crying, and he would be thinking about the time passing. Why was it taking so long?

Adding to the strangeness, he had not been on a plane since he had flown out of Beirut with Nadine, sitting in first class with her serving him good Bordeaux in her red uniform. Why was everything taking so long?

New York

Gone a year, almost broke and living over his head just off the Plaza Mayor in Madrid, he thought he had no choice but to limp home, but then lucked into a job with the Associated Press in New York. When he called Irma from 50 Rockefeller Plaza to let her know, she pointed out that she had not heard from him over that same year. She said she missed knowing what he was up to. He had never heard that from her.

When he began to apologize she interrupted, telling him she liked New York. Bob had been stationed briefly at the Naval Air Station there—at Floyd Bennett Field.

"When was that?"

"Before you were born."

"What year? What were you doing?"

"Hard to remember exactly."

"Why is that?"

"You weren't born yet."

None of the women he met in New York were interested in having babies. They liked politics and other women who liked politics. They liked their careers, no matter how frustrating. Like him, he figured. The women a few years older were . . . *superior* was the word he used to compliment them. They did not call themselves *badass* like some of the women that came later, but they would take him on in unexpected ways—pinching his ass when he was shooting the first Women's March up Fifth Avenue.

That march was barely news, page thirty in the *Times*, but with a strong piece by Grace Lichtenstein characterizing the marchers as young, white, and middle class, chanting, "sisterhood is powerful," and carrying banners that read *Crush Phallic Imperialism* and *Pills for Men*. He liked the signs, and worked to get them into his shots.

Bands of feminists conducted "guerrilla actions" by showing up in numbers at various institutions, including the First National City Bank, the IRS, and St. Patrick's Cathedral. At a rally on the Central Park Mall at Seventy-Second Street, a group of women announced, "We lesbians no longer allow the title to be negative." There were lots of lesbians, more than he had expected. He liked them too.

At the American Stock Exchange, other women unfurled a twelve foot *Woman Power* banner from the visitors' gallery above the trading floor. Traders looked up and jeered, making obscene gestures at the banner. Escorted out by guards, the women then marched down Wall Street to the New York Stock Exchange, shouting, "We can't bear any more bull." Hecklers shouted back, "Go home and wash the dishes," and other suggestions, mostly about fucking. For about an hour, the women stood with their banner on the steps of the Federal Hall National Memorial as a large, hostile, largely male crowd gathered. The men reminded him of Norm, the way he would look women over and then give them a hard time, even Irma.

Afterward, the women, followed by a parade of reporters and photographers, staged "bar-ins" at restaurants that refused to serve unescorted women at their bars. His favorite sign was *Women on Top*. The women liked that one too. He remembered the anger of women at SDS meetings making a big deal out of refusing to make the coffee. These women were different, more fun, *liberating* even.

He dropped off his film, and he went back to one of the bars.

LA

After a couple years in New York, he was back in California working as a reporter on a weekly newspaper start-up. Irma had meanwhile stacked up enough summer school credits for a master's degree. She sent him an announcement from San Jose State listing her as a new Master of Primary Education. When he called to congratulate her, she surprised him by asking what he was writing besides his journalism. Like what? he wondered . . .

"Maybe something like the writers you like," Irma volunteered.

"Maybe in a couple years," he told her.

"Are you still painting?" she asked.

He wondered if she remembered his becoming a *painter of ideas*. That still embarrassed him. And why he was not an artist was a question he had put away. He did not explain but said he was flattered she had asked about both his writing and his art.

"You're a better writer," Irma continued. "You can still paint for fun."

For fun? That had never occurred to him. They hung up.

He was a journalist now, and that was that. But he still followed the art scene and met Chris Burden, who was scaring critics with dangerous, sometimes hard-to-watch performance pieces, starting with "Shoot," at a gallery in Santa Ana where he had an anonymous artist friend shoot him in the arm with a small-caliber rifle. "As American as apple pie," Burden said.

They both lived on Ocean Front Walk in Venice, and Burden had gone to UC Irvine, so they had the young minimalists in common too. He pitched a profile of Burden to *Esquire*, got the assignment, and, to give the story a jolt of New Journalism, they collaborated on a piece Burden called *747*.

Early one morning in late September they met at Dockweiler State Park, where he photographed Burden firing a pistol at a rising Boeing 747 from the deserted beach under its LAX flight path. He was the only witness, and he made his image from behind, with Burden's shooting arm at a forty-five-degree angle into the sky. The plane's shape was clear and it seemed safely out of range, but maybe not.

It was difficult to get the 747 big enough in the frame to be recognizable as more than a speck over Burden's shoulder. If he got that right, it would make the piece. If not, it was just a troubling picture of a man with a gun. When they were walking back to their cars, an LAPD cruiser pulled up on the cliff above the wide beach, but then drove away.

They had breakfast in a booth at the Hinano Cafe in Venice. Burden gave him a release to sign, relinquishing all rights to the images. No big deal. Burden looked exhausted, hammered down. He tried to empathize, but thinking about what they had just done had a kick to it. It was hilarious, actually, now that it turned out not to have been criminally foolish. This encouraged comparisons to other follies, all funny the way failures can be funny, but then Burden was a long way from *Don Quixote*. More like *Ubu Roi*, or maybe Soupy Sales. Art was ideas, anyway. This was what he would write for *Esquire*. Dada, dada, dada . . . They ordered breakfast beers. He rewound his Nikon and handed over the film.

He sent *Esquire* what he thought were seven thousand disciplined words that pulled together everything he knew about conceptual art and the new LA art scene, with Burden at the center with lightning shooting out of his ears. Weeks passed without a response. Always a bad sign.

Finally a note saying they were cutting the piece back, but he would get his full fee. What ran two months later were 250 words in the annual Dubious Achievements cover package describing "Shoot" under a grainy, full-page black-and-white photo of Burden looking confused, with a .22 hole in his left arm. His words were deadpan, but the display copy and positioning were snide. *What a dumb fuck to have somebody shoot him and call it art. Ha ha ha.*

He was angry and embarrassed. Burden was not mad or even annoyed. They met at a bar in Santa Monica.

"You're in the wrong business," Burden said, calling for another drink.

San Francisco

Irma had always encouraged him to learn to write well, but never *something like the writers you like*. She had changed something in him with that. Click. *Sometimes you think something is enough for you, but then maybe not.* He *did* want to be that kind of writer. He was immediately, surprisingly happy, his new motivation kindling reassuring images.

He remembered when he wanted to be a forest ranger, which was right after fighter pilot and buckaroo. He was feeling older but fidgety. Irma saw this, and they sat on the cinder-block step. She told him to imagine everything he could about the life he wanted, then become the person he needed to be to live that life. He got it. To be a forest ranger he needed a tent.

Irma smiled.

He quit journalism and moved to San Francisco to write a novel. He wore Levi's, rough-out cowboy boots, and a corduroy sport jacket with leather patches on the elbows. He cultivated a combination of toughness and sensitivity, wanting to write with integrity and make literature in a manly way. He knew it was a pose but had not considered where he had picked it up or where it might lead.

Always somewhere in his mind was Irma encouraging him: *something like the writers you like.*

The writers he liked then were Pynchon and DeLillo and Wolfe, and he was never going to touch them, but he wrote every day, trying things. His novel was unhinged, coming to him like a banging door in the back of his head. It was about a teenage girl raped in Gold Rush California and her trail of revenge as she grows into womanhood. That it was a comic novel underlined how far he could stray. His working title was *The 49er.*

He got to one hundred pages fast, but no agent or publisher got back to him. He had no car, a Ducati 350 instead. He loved that bike, the way he could slide through traffic like a snake. Dangerous in the rain, though, and winter was coming. He had no money and a shitty apartment on California Street. Women were not interested. He would tell them his heroes were Yossarian from *Catch-22* and Crazy Horse and what did they think of that? They had nothing to say to him.

Being unattractive to women unnerved him. He was forlorn. He missed the stir. He needed money. He got an editing job at a magazine start-up by showing off during his interview with fifty story ideas on three-by-five cards. It was assumed he had editing experience. No matter. Now he was an editor. He got to make some decisions. He would ride that to a career, but when he walked into the office his first day, he had no idea what to do. Then he did. Irma was right, he did not have to talk all the time to get people to listen to him.

She had taught him how to listen, and now he would work hard and concentrate. He learned to insert himself into problems, fix them quickly or move on immediately. Look for whatever would make the highest impact, adjust the small stuff along the way. He found it advantageous to be candid about his mistakes, volunteering how this or that needed to be improved, and then spraying ideas around like he was marking territory. That was the job, the work. He was in it for *the work*. Take it or leave it. He remembered Christmas Eve on Irma's porch. That is what he was figuring out.

Manhattan

He never told anyone where he was from or about Irma or who Norm was, but they were always somewhere in his mind, distant but interrupting like prairie storms he knew from Wyoming, seeming random, then not—Norm lying to Irma about running his Cadillac off the road. He hated that, but there was nothing more to say. He had gotten out of there.

It was a long reach from Manhattan in the '80s back to the Santa Clara Valley of the '50s, and being from California was not particularly useful or cool, and he no longer wrapped himself in it. Sometimes, though, he would sense how naive he might be. He did not wear cowboy boots to work or make a big deal out of Mexican food, but confrontation with an establishment he was unprepared for ran him into authority he had problems with—hard doors. He picked up the media shorthand and was not dented by the insecurity of, say, not getting into Smith or Harvard or Stanford or all the way down to Wesleyan or wherever, but he did not fit in.

He fought to be included in meetings and surprised himself with ambition that he could not trace except somehow to Irma teaching him to love California—land of two-thousand-year-old sequoias, where things happened fast, where contradictions were welcome. Well, maybe his ambition was his contradiction. Maybe that was what he was feeling.

He remembered Irma telling him everything would become more interesting if he slowed down once in a while. He slowed down, and walked to work for the first time in his life. New York City became increasingly compelling even as he remembered the passing trees out the window of Irma's Ford when he was riding in cabs. He could feel the uncertainty of whatever was coming next, but he trusted the chaos. What he did not yet understand was that, like Irma, he was drawn to the seam, the edge between what was wild and what was not.

Looking through binoculars from the twenty-ninth-floor *Rolling Stone* office on Fifth Avenue, he could see down on the 1,200-pound polar bear who spent his days pacing back and forth in a cage in the Central Park Zoo. The bear, whose name was Scandy, would rub his face on the bars in one corner then, swinging his big body, turn back in the other direction, moving purposefully, and repeat the rubbing with his nose between the bars when he reached the far corner. He had a dark stripe from his right eye down his nose where he had rubbed his fur off to a polished scar. Visiting the great bear became part of living in New York for him, even though he was always saddened by the hopelessness.

When he mentioned Scandy to Irma, she told him that when she was a little girl on the farm in Solon Springs they had a dog who started barking one day and would not stop. The dog had been chained to a stake in front of the chicken coop to keep foxes away.

That was how the dog lived, on a twenty-foot chain. She remembered several years when the dog did not bark, and then the week when the dog would not stop until Fronie could not stand it any longer and shot him with her deer rifle.

He did not know what to say to that. Irma said she should not have told him. He asked what the dog's name was. She was silent for a moment. On second thought, it was probably a story he needed to know. And the dog's name was Buddy.

Buddy was still in his head some months later when a man his age described as "homeless and irrational" was mauled to death by Scandy inside his cage. The young man had been noticed the previous afternoon, carrying a garbage bag of his possessions, going up to cages, trying to get closer to animals. Park police told him to leave. When he returned that night, almost five hours after the zoo had closed, he was spotted by a night watchman and again led out of the zoo. At three a.m., he was spotted near the lion cages. As he was led out that time, the man said, "Help me." But when the watchman offered to take him to a shelter, he turned away, dragging his garbage bag.

The newspaper stories noted multiple wounds to the head, neck, chest, and arms. The man had scaled a series of fences to get inside the six-hundred-square-foot cage. Once he had dropped to the ground, the inward curving bars made it impossible to get out. His body was discovered early the next morning lying partly in a pool of bloody water. Scandy was watching from a few feet away in one of his corners.

Zookeepers said Scandy had done what a normal bear would do to defend its territory. Scandy was not all that happy in the first place, as indicated by his endless pacing and the black scar. The animal psychologist consulted said bears did not suffer from depression, and perhaps Scandy was just bored.

He would have to think about that, but not as hard as he thought about Fronie aiming her deer rifle.

Extra Mustard

He called Irma to wish her happy birthday and wound up telling her he was not sure about his job. She said if he was looking out his office window at the Sherry-Netherland hotel—as he had just bragged—it had to be better than shoveling asphalt.

Since he had started working at what Irma never called his *career*, they had a new dynamic, a kind of code. Nothing was ever wrong in their lives. No complaints from either of them. When they talked about people they had known in Burbank or Campbell, there was no judgment. He was aware of this turn in their relationship as a way to create a better past in the face of regret. But regret was never Irma's style, so it was probably him trying to hide the sinking confidence he was feeling again, like the winter fog on Irma's porch. Now she was teaching by example. He did not have to criticize anyone.

On that same birthday call, Irma told him about an essay she had written when she was a junior in high school in Solon Springs. The topic was, "What I Want to Be." She had wanted to be a stenographer and she was going to go to secretarial school and study as hard as she could to be a good one. That was all she wanted in the world, but writing the essay had embarrassed her at the time. He did not know where she was going with that.

"But then you went to college," he said lamely.

"I changed my mind."

She was giving him advice.

"I wanted more," Irma said.

A month later, he went to *Newsweek*, and was immediately drawn to Katharine Graham, who owned the magazine as well as the *Washington Post*. Top editors called her Kay, but he introduced himself addressing her as Mrs. Graham, and she seemed to appreciate that. Irma's manners, he thought to himself, and became comfortable calling her Kay soon enough.

Kay liked extra mustard on her hot dogs, and so did he—which he learned when he offered to get more for the two of them poolside at a corporate retreat in Puerto Rico. She could be imperious and then drop *shithead* into a description of a US senator. He liked that too, how searing it sounded in her refined, moneyed voice.

Seeing Kay raise a hand to absently touch an earring reminded him of Irma. Kay and Irma, born the same year, 1917, both Lutheran, both married in 1940, both with dead husbands. Kay was raised between a country estate near Mount Kisco, New York, and a mansion in Washington, DC, while Irma grew up on a farm without indoor plumbing in rural Wisconsin, but there was a sameness he recognized. They both paid attention. They asked him what he thought.

When he told Irma about Kay, he said they wore their hair the same way. Irma did not seem to care about that. She said it would be nice to be in charge, and then told him there were no women principals in the Campbell Union School District. Bingo. Irma was a feminist. How could that surprise him? He knew that long before he knew the word. His whole life he had seen her strength—working, making her own way.

Irma even looked like Gloria Steinem, which he told her when he gave her a subscription to *Ms. Magazine*. She already knew who Gloria was, and told him in a surprisingly formal thank-you note that *Ms.* was interesting and she agreed with almost everything she read in it. He wondered what she did not agree with but knew they were never going to talk about that. The river jetty came back to him, like a raw February wind blowing off the water, the *shedding of skin*.

Irma

Someone named Irma Elden on line two," his secretary said.

He would remember this as the only time Irma called him at any of his offices. She called to tell him she was moving over the hill to Santa Cruz. Not to Pleasure Point, where she loved the view from the cliff, but a few miles south and a mile inland. She had the money, and she had had enough of Campbell. Then she asked him something she had never asked.

"Do you have a girlfriend?"

Parade

When he was in junior high school, Irma told him if he liked girls they would like him back, and they did. Now he liked women, and was drawn to women others found difficult. They were more interesting simply by not going along, sometimes busting him for not paying attention or showing off. Like Irma, in a way, but, of course, not. He was aware that women not letting him off the hook for this or that might be good for him, might be helping him *evolve*, in the argot of the day.

Little by little, he started listening more carefully to them. One told him the greatest gift you can give a lover is the thought that you are both alive at the same time. Proust, he thought. She smiled sweetly at him and explained Joyce's thinking that a good enough writer could awaken the experience of being alive every moment. He loved that.

Another woman told him he was just one more float in the parade.

Fair enough. Plus, it cracked women up when he told the parade story. He knew he was being provocative, which always reminded him that Irma did not like it when he was provocative—which his teachers sometimes noted as a disciplinary problem on his report cards. Irma talked to him about it. She told him only ideas should be provocative.

"Do you have any ideas?"

Not then, he didn't.

He became a student of his flirtations, but was less aware than he thought. He knew different women and what they were like, but did not know what *he* was like, and he is writing here about a time when his actual experience seemed to him without context, a time when he hit on women on airplanes and went home with bartenders, living almost entirely without plans. Hiding now in the autobiographical third person does not really change anything.

All he could recall about the curator who knocked on his door at the Hay-Adams after a reception in Washington for a painter friend was that she was not embarrassed to be naked in front of him. He wished now they had been sober. This came back to him when #MeToo finally hit, and he saw so many men shivering in anticipation of being called out for behavior they said they could not remember. He wondered what the curator remembered.

A woman he knew vaguely in California had just moved to New York and he invited her to lunch. It was spring. They met at an outdoor table at the café at the Stanhope Hotel. Across the street, the fountains of the Metropolitan Museum shot water into the air. She was wearing a light cotton dress. He remembered her as very serious about her career. She told him San Francisco was easier, but New York had *momentum*. She liked that.

He nodded.

"It saves time," she said.

He liked that, and the more he thought about it the more he liked her, but he said nothing.

"What?" she asked. She was not testing him exactly, more like she knew there was something else on his mind.

"It occurs to me I'm not up to you."

She smiled and held up a small vial. "Let's find out."

In bed the next morning, she laughed when the bells of a nearby church started tolling in the middle of his orgasm. He thought he might write about those bells someday but was not at all sure what he would write. It had to be about more than just him and his penis, and good luck with that, anyway. There was too much to get wrong.

Manners

He was playing catch-up in the middle of what was not yet understood to be the second wave of feminism—the Women's Liberation Movement. Every woman he liked was all for it. They marched. They did not burn their bras, but many stopped wearing them. He liked to be around these women, especially the ones a little older than he was. They reminded him of Irma in ways he did not quite recognize. What had Irma been like at their age, in her thirties? She had gotten rid of Norm, for one thing.

There was new feminist theory that the best men were raised by strong mothers, and that the lack of close, early mother-son connections caused sexism and destructive masculinity. If he told the women he knew about Irma, they said he was lucky. The most ideological said women like Irma were central to blowing up both traditional masculinity and the larger patriarchal culture. No argument from him.

It's not as if his best friends were women, but some of them were. And no question he depended on women up and down his various mastheads. Not that they could move up that masthead and take his job, an unfairness unrecognized until years later, when women were no longer embarrassed if this made them angry.

Irma was like that, hiding what had to be her frustration with the superintendent of the Campbell Union School District, especially following her disappointments in Norm.

Men had all the power. Told the same jokes, like Norm's favorite, the one about a young bull and an old bull on a hill, looking down on a pasture of cows. He was never going to tell that joke, but he was never going to forget it either.

One time, when a woman he brought to a work reception was flippant with a board member, the guy pulled him aside. "I can see you haven't fucked her yet," the guy said, grinning, like Norm's wisecracking about women asking for whatever they got. He looked hard at the guy until the woman pulled him back to her, mocking the smirk on the guy's face. He should have said something right then, or at least called the guy on it later. It was not a coin flip, simply what Irma called *the right thing*. High school came back. Clydia humiliated by his teammate, his own silence, his cowardice. It made him feel weak and emasculated—a stupid irony. Now, by not sticking up for his date, he had memorialized it, still hearing Frankie Valli in his head.

Irma had told him that standing whenever a woman entered the room was really about him. So was opening doors and carrying bags of groceries. Manners were important to Irma, and he liked his manners. Every woman he knew liked them too. Mrs. Graham. But none of that was about him anymore. Much of what he thought of as benign details of his adventures with the women he liked, often playing the rascal, were affronts to the dignity of those women way beyond bad manners. He would come to see that.

He had always liked to be told he looked good and assumed

women did too. Women he knew made jokes about their *fuck me* pumps, how steep and uncomfortable they were. He told a girl-friend that the only thing good about her leaving was watching her walk away. She said it turned her on thinking about that, thinking about him watching her, but he should never assume. He had to be invited, but then was drink-and-dial ever a good idea, even if you were invited over?

He knew what happened in his office—to colleagues, cleaning staff, women in tailored suits snapping down the hall in $1,200 heels. Women were always aware of it, and it was always creepy. He never leered, but he thought about women all the time. He assumed all men were like that, lusting randomly, always horny— Norm, rolling a toothpick in his mouth and winking to him that a girl in his seventh-grade class was stacked.

He had always been proud that everyone said Irma was the pretti-est mom, but he remembered one time back in Duluth when he was very young and she was talking on the phone. They were dressed up to go out and he was standing next to her, waiting in his little bow tie, and she was telling her girlfriend, Sis, that it was never good to be *too* pretty. Why he remembered that so clearly was no longer confusing. The thing was, though, he had always known there was something wrong, even if it was complicated by details he had somehow missed only to remember now.

Irma

As an editor, especially at *Esquire*, it was useful to appear enlightened about women's issues. He was not cynical about this. It seemed obvious, although it was sometimes received with snideness: *Gee, isn't Esquire a men's magazine?*

Well, exactly.

In a particular editor's letter, he wrote that as a little boy he knew that little girls had the intelligence and energy he had, but then, in adolescence, he got to go wild and girls did not, which turned them inward with their problems because the message they got everywhere was to just be nice. If girls did not shut up and look good, they were tagged whiners or worse, and suffered much more emotional distress, discrimination, poverty, and physical abuse than boys.

He thought Irma would like what he wrote and mailed her a proof before the magazine was off press. When he called her, she said it was a nice surprise. She was now dating Carl, a publishing executive at the San Jose *Mercury News*, and Carl had told her it was shrewd, as in a good business move.

"Thank Carl," he said. "But I wasn't thinking about it that way." The moment he lied, he knew Irma would know.

"Good," Irma said, "because it's true."

"What I wrote?"

"It's harder for every one of them than it ever was for you."

"I know."

"Probably not."

When they hung up, he wondered what had just happened. They had never had a conversation like that. It was the closest she had ever come to spanking him.

Stir

One cold spring in New York, a strikingly thin woman told him she was still in shock from her divorce, but was now, finally, deservingly, rich. She raised a hand to her Cartier necklace. They smiled at each other. She explained what a catch she would be—classy and connected, fun in the sack, even sweet when she was being what she called *herself*. He was in her bed, anxious to leave. She lit a cigarette and told him their history was all fucked up.

"I think you know that," she said, putting the cigarette out immediately. Her eyes were suddenly swimming. She said she did not want to go over the same old stuff. He told her she would be with someone else, forgetting about him, soon enough.

That was how it worked, the dynamic. Lovers tired of each other. A drama major he lived with in college started seeing one of her professors while they were still living together. A television producer in San Francisco dumped him for her riding instructor. A photographer in New York said he was crowding her and moved back to Kenya. An American in Milan did not like it when he frowned in his sleep. An ironic poet at a writer's conference said he was too ironic. They all moved on. Just like him.

———

He had another, much older memory from Newport Beach. When his teacher friend and he were new to each other, they would sometimes walk up the beach to the river jetty to watch the sunset. She had a straw cowboy hat she had picked up in Nebraska, and she wore it on their walks. They would share a joint and he would talk elliptically about conceptual art. In the middle of one of those conversations she stopped walking and told him she wanted to be clear.

"You're not right for me," she said. "Let's just enjoy each other."

Fine, but he did not understand, and looking back now, what had happened when she became pregnant was cloudy. He still felt bad about the way things ended, but that was a long time ago. Who had he been then? His memory disappointed him. He read that when more and more information fills your brain, you have less control over what you remember. Obvious. What he remembered was her hat—good straw with a rodeo crease, a tight-rolled brim, sweat stains under the band with a small turkey feather, and a slide strap. He loved that hat.

Wives

When he was ten, Margo from next door told him she was going to let him marry her when they were grown-up. When he told Irma, she smiled and told him Margo was a very smart girl but he should take his time with that. He knew she was teasing him, but for the next thirty years he never came close to marrying anyone. In the vernacular of those decades, he was *not ready*. He was not waiting for something to sing in his blood, in talk, or in bed. People made love or they fucked. Both fine with him, but he was always backing out of rooms, avoiding commitment.

He could have counted the happy marriages he knew then on one hand. None from when he was growing up. He had understood as a little boy that marriages were fragile. When they lived in Burbank, he wanted to tell Irma how it was bad for him with Norm, but he never said anything because he did not want to ruin Irma's marriage. The dark side of marriage—betrayal, shouts coming through bedroom walls, violence—was not an abstraction for him, but as he grew older he did not identify with it. He knew Irma was a good wife and that in the end he would be a good husband. Not if, when. Maybe Irma had taught him to believe in love after all.

———

Irma had three husbands, and in photographs they looked enough alike to be cousins, especially in their uniforms. He had two wives, one dark, one light, and very different women in almost every way, but both beautiful. He was faithful to them and tried to do what they asked, even when he thought it was not necessarily what they wanted or needed. He did this because he had once heard Irma telling a friend that a good marriage was about *bending a little*.

He met his first wife at a Midtown bar where she had invited him for a drink. She was a book editor and had heard he knew so-called Western Writers. Western writers, especially from Montana, were enjoying an unanticipated popularity among New York editors. Although he did not think of himself as a Montana Writer, he did have a place in the Paradise Valley, where he had moved to finish that still-unhinged novel he had started in San Francisco. The novel was now about to be published, and he had taken a job at *Rolling Stone*. He was not sure how she knew all that, but she did.

There were people she wanted him to meet. She knew everyone. They started seeing a lot of each other, staying up late. He slept over. It was dramatic and compelling until at some point it was inevitable . . . Here is where his memory fades off, closes down, blanks out.

They were married six weeks later, above an ice cream shop on the main street in Cody, Wyoming. There was no ceremony. By Wyoming law, the justice of the peace asks the bride if she is there under duress; if she says no, the couple is married. They spent that night at the Irma Hotel, named for Buffalo Bill's daughter.

He called Irma from the pay phone in the bar to tell her. Before she picked up, he wondered what she would say, surprised by his trepidation. He almost hung up. A premonition? He hoped not. Irma's marriage to Norm had been a justice-of-the-peace deal like his a couple hours ago, but in the middle of the night in Carson City with him asleep in the back seat of the Ford in a casino parking lot.

"Well," Irma said, when she finally answered. "I'm sure you'll get to know each other."

When they did, the marriage disintegrated. She was too sophisticated for him, and they never seemed to have enough money. Their good years were followed by mutual frustrations tempered only by preoccupation with their two sons. In strange, misguided deference to the boys, they did not divorce when he moved out. He saved her angry letters out of bitterness and to warn his sons, then threw them away.

He was still married when he met his second wife but had been living single for many years. When he moved in with her on Abingdon Square, he would sit by her front window writing and drinking late into the night. He imagined he could see her life—how it was and how it might be with him in it. Out her window, he would see a young woman walking home alone or with someone she had probably just met and he would ache to be with her that way. To have been young with her. He pictured them as husband and wife, paintings in separate frames that would hang together, side by side, like the portraits of minor Italian royalty in those small palaces in the Lake Region.

They talked about their childhoods, seemingly somehow parallel. For him, there was the sadness of not having known his father, knowing Norm instead. She knew that same sadness, but in her own way. She told him about stringy hair and bad clothes. Her parents were older and didn't understand. They drank. He knew the embarrassment of their drunkenness. He admired her for the deals she had made, the deals she had had to make to get from there to here as a woman, to live on her own terms. In the back of his mind, he knew Irma would have liked that.

So maybe it was fate, something he did not believe in except in the moments between them that followed. What did he want his life to be? She had the same question.

Pleasure Point

Irma called to tell him she was going to marry Carl, who was retiring from the paper. They had both worked since they were kids,
and were going to take it easy for a while, play a little golf, support
the San Francisco Symphony and the new aquarium in Monterey.
Carl lived near her in an old beachfront cottage. Irma had traded
up with the four houses she had bought and sold and now owned a
sprawling split-level in La Selva Beach that looked out on artichoke
fields and the ocean beyond. They were going to sell both and get
something on the cliff above Pleasure Point.

"Pleasure Point," Irma said again.

2

(SONS)

Little boys want to be men like their fathers even if that father is dead. That had been him as Irma's son, thinking (letting people think) he was raising himself.

As a father, he wanted to make amends for the wrongness of that.

Fatherless Father

He was in the water, looking back at his sons on the beach. A rented summerhouse rose against the sky behind them. One was sleeping on his stomach, his perfect back glowing in the late sun. The other sat reading. They were young still, eight and ten, but time was passing.

He had no philosophy of fatherhood, only specifics going back—a bee sting in Texas, that tiny scarlet hourglass on a black widow in Willow Glen. His sons needed to see the details, to find them in their own lives, and to look at the hard things too—his torn arm in that emergency room when he was seven. Irma's wisdom. That is where the lesions would be for them as their time passed. They would fall out of trees.

Nick, the oldest, was born at three thirty in the afternoon without complication. The shiny February light out the hospital window seemed to polish the starkness of the bare trees. When he called Irma from a hospital phone, she told him he had been born in the afternoon too. Twenty-six months later, at six thirty in the morning, Thomas was born with his lungs collapsing. Dressed in scrubs, he watched his new son gasping for life in the ICU. Eighteen hours later, when the doctors had assured him, he walked home wondering if Thomas would remember.

They lived at 7 Gracie Square then, on the Upper East Side of Manhattan. It was a solid prewar building, facing a small park, which ran along the East River. Some of the building's co-ops had views of the Roosevelt Island Lighthouse and the Triborough Bridge, but they lived in the back, looking south. The only view of the river was from the boys' room. In the middle of the night he would watch them sleeping. Out the window he saw boats running on the flat water, their lights approximating the supernatural.

As a new father he brooded about inherited weakness, and tried to be a good father to please his own dead father. He did not think about it that way at the time, but when the boys were older and trying to please him, he knew that the person whose approval he wanted most had never been there. That was the war, the waste. Irma's sadness.

His young sons consumed his attention. He worried about their formulas and pediatricians and preschools. He wheeled them in strollers to the children's zoo in Central Park to name the animals. They camped out on the beach in a new tent. There was an electric train around the Christmas tree. As they got older, he took them everywhere with him. Fatherhood seemed to be a good fit, but he began to worry about too many birthday presents and what he was teaching them, besides how to treat a snakebite and other Boy Scout knowledge they would probably never use.

He wondered sometimes if Irma had been as preoccupied with him, but she had had no choice. He also wondered if she had worried about spoiling him. Well, she *had* spoiled him, but never in ways that he would come to expect special treatment. The love he felt from her did not make him more dependent and timid; somehow it made him stronger and more independent. That is what he wanted for his sons.

On Easter Sunday when Thomas was seven or eight, they went to a fancy lawn party in Amagansett. It was a routine social event for the parents, mostly media and music people, but with an elaborate egg hunt for the many children who had been invited with their parents. When the hunt started, the older children fanned out quickly, whooping whenever they found one of the numerous perfect, brightly colored eggs. There was also a special golden egg, which was the biggest prize of all.

He was standing with the host when Thomas wandered over, looking frustrated.

"How are you doing?" the host asked.

Thomas shrugged and showed his empty basket. The host nodded toward a planter behind them. The golden egg was on the mowed grass behind the planter. Thomas picked it up hesitantly and then ran off to join the other children.

"He looked like he needed that," said the host.

He thanked the host.

On the way home in the car, Thomas told him he did not want to lie about finding the egg, but he did not want to tell on the host either. He did not like the way any of that felt. "Turned me into a liar," Thomas said.

"Good for Thomas," Irma said, when he told her what had happened.

Captains

On a fishing trip to Guatemala that came through his magazine job, he spent the flight down explaining to his sons how his fishing as a boy had been for bluegills, with Irma showing him how to dig for worms and bait a hook. He sometimes told his sons about parts of his childhood, but never anything about Norm. He figured they were having a hard enough time with his separation from their mother without having to think about his problems at their age.

The airport in Guatemala City was full of state police with M4s, but the civil war had ended the previous year and their three days on the water were filled with wonder at where they were and what they were doing. It was the fish, of course, but also the water, the deep blue descending into an eternity off the stern of a thirty-one-foot, twin-diesel Gamefisher. He watched his sons closely, hoping the mysteries of all the cruising fish in all the oceans in the world would point to the mysteries of their own small lives catching these beautiful fish. A sailfish on light tackle felt electric, energy surging straight back up your line, and if you got one to the boat, it glowed a neon silver-blue.

Their captain was said to have caught and released two thousand billfish in a single year, and the boys were enthralled when he let them steer, standing next to him on the flying bridge. He joked that maybe they would become charter captains like him, join the brotherhood who fish the Pacific, usually for marlin from home ports in South America, California, and in their captain's case, Hawaii. It was a wild, free life, and now that word had gotten out about the sensational new sailfish grounds off Guatemala, a handful of captains had come to cash in on the new six-week season.

The lodge owner suggested that he host a dinner for the captains to promote both his magazine and the lodge—and to return the favor of the discount he was getting on the trip. There would be seven captains, several with guests. Fine, until they were all seated and two of the guests turned out to be local girls the captains had hired to live with them for the short season—both pretty and too young. Nick and Thomas were confused at first. They knew girls that age at home. The captains' girls saw this and lowered their eyes. The captains were boisterous, calling for large rum drinks. He saw one wink at Nick. The owner shrugged at him.

He stood up at the head of the table and said they had a very early flight, gave a short toast to the wonders of Guatemalan waters, and took the boys to eat in their room. They did not talk about it that night, or in the morning. He wanted to tell them that he did not know what they had been walking into and that they would understand when they were older. But what was it they would understand? That Captain's wink as something in common, solidarity, corruption—Norm, rolling a toothpick in his mouth?

All he really knew was that you can think you are done with something, and it will come back at a different time and you can see it in a different way if you want. Usually some kind of justification. On the way to the airport, when he started to talk to his sons about the captains, Nick cut him off, saying they understood. Thomas nodded. They were angry. Nick said next time they would rather go fishing for bluegills with Irma.

Dead Letters

Soon after they had arrived in California, Irma told him Bob wrote beautiful letters that she would show him one day, but she never did, and he still wondered in what way they were beautiful.

He thought about Bob's letters every Father's Day, when he wrote to his own sons that they made him so rich of spirit that the emptiness of not knowing his own father was filled with the great joy of knowing them. He got that from Irma, who always thanked him for whatever Mother's Day gift he had made for her at school by telling him about some wonderful time they had had together when he was younger—like when she had taken him to a carnival at Park Point in Duluth and there were pony rides and she put him on a pony and the pony had started bucking and he had laughed and laughed.

Writing to his sons he recounted stroller trips to the Children's Zoo, where a certain duck always chased them and they would laugh and laugh and shout out, "Grouchy Duck!" As they grew older, he laid out plans for road trips and reminded them how they had started collecting maps together. They knew all the capitals, like Irma had taught him, before it was time to learn them in school.

On their birthdays, Irma sent them books. Their letters back to her were more complicated than he expected, often telling her something that he had said or done. Thomas also drew on his letters, colorful cartoons depicting adventures with his brother. Thomas often put him in the drawings too, or the drawings were only of him with a huge head. Looking into this, he read that a child may be suffering from insecurity that anticipates depression and other emotional problems if he draws one person much larger than himself. He asked Irma about this, and she said it was normal. "You drew pictures like that of me all the time," she said. "But Thomas draws much better than you ever did."

When he sent Irma their report cards, she always wrote back to them, never to him. She wrote she was proud of them but grades were not everything. What were they reading? When he wondered about this, Irma told him he had never cared about grades except to show off, like he was doing now with his sons' report cards.

"They care," Irma said, "maybe a little too much."

Long silence.

On his own birthdays, when the boys had become teenagers, he considered writing letters to be read after his death. Perhaps they could find the lessons he had wanted for himself at their age, a toughness they could feel inside when they trusted themselves. Never mind that it might spook them, or that Irma had never pulled anything like that on him.

He was in strong physical health on each of the birthdays that he sat down to write the two letters he actually finished. His sons were away at school by then, and the letters were never sent—remaining wherever he stuck them in a now-forgotten book. Neither letter started with anything like *If you're reading this, I'm dead*, but that was the idea. He believed the instinct to do this was connected to Bob leaving him before he had any chance of acquiring Bob's wisdom. What wisdom that might have been was not something he thought about, probably because Irma's wisdom was always there with him, direct and obvious every time he called on it.

When he was starting a new school in the second grade, Irma drove him early on her way to her own school. Most of the mothers went into the classroom to meet the teacher, but Irma already knew her, so she was just dropping him off. He was quiet in the car. Irma asked him what he was thinking. After a moment he said very slowly that he did not want to make any mistakes. He was afraid of going in alone. Irma said he would feel better if he thought about who he was. He did exactly that until Irma pulled up in front of his new school and reached across him to open the passenger door.

"You can do this," she said. "We both know you can."

That is what he wanted his letters to his sons to be about, and he wanted them to know from his first lines what they had in front of them. He got that from Irma too.

Wyoming

Irma did not come east to meet his sons when they were born, and he did not take them to California to meet Irma until she lived at Pleasure Point. In retrospect, they both considered those decisions mistakes, but by then they were resigned to a visit every other summer. It was not as if they shared some kind of convergent evolution, finding their own ways to solve similar problems of parenthood. He simply followed Irma's lead and tried to make the best of things.

When he came into the world as the first grandson, it had been a very big deal, but of course he had been replacing Bob. "Little Terry" was fussed over and observed closely for signs of being *just like Bob*, probably until Irma had to get out of there. Now, observing his own sons, he became aware that every childhood has an emotional geography to be negotiated.

Thinking about this made him more aware of how Irma had handled him, gotten him through—although she never accepted any credit for him turning out more or less okay. At least he was not going to wind up twitchy with drugs or with his life totaled like his Ducati on a winter road in Marin.

———

There had been a woman in Wyoming, a rancher's daughter, who showed him how a new colt can stand after only thirty minutes, and begin to take shaky steps. His mare will lean into him, teaching him to lean back on her as he learns to walk. In about two hours, the colt will trot and then gallop. He told Irma about this on the phone from Dubois.

"You were like that for me," he said, half teasing, intending a compliment.

She told him flatly she was glad he could ride. "We had horses on the farm," she said. "It's not just the colts."

So, another lesson . . . Yes, fillies. And never take yourself too seriously, especially with romantic ideas that are mostly full of bologna. He got it. And it was interesting that mares were good mothers, but why exhaust yourself thinking about tricks of scientific abstraction—like DNA? He got that too. Then, out of nowhere, surprising himself, he asked Irma if she had ever fired Fronie's deer rifle.

"During deer season," Irma said, "whenever she'd let me hunt." Irma paused.

"I forgot about that," she said finally.

Running Fence

When his sons were old enough to be interested in such things, they would ask about their religion. They never went to church. What were they? He said they were *animists*. They belonged to nature.

On a trip to visit Irma at her new house at Pleasure Point, he took them to the giant redwood groves in Big Basin. Some of the trees were fifty feet around and more than a football field high. He said Irma had brought him there when he was their age and told him it was like visiting a great cathedral. From then on he had looked for places like that for himself, and they should too.

That night Irma made tacos and showed them how to spin flour tortillas without burning their fingers. It struck him as he looked around her new house that except for that one Currier & Ives print in Campbell he could remember no art from his childhood. He also realized there had been no paintings in Irma's various houses until she started collecting seascapes that matched the view out her windows at Pleasure Point. The seascapes were almost clichéd, but he liked them.

Irma told him to skip the tacos and go to dinner with an old friend from high school who had just called. When he returned, he found the three of them sitting together on the floor in front of the big windows that looked out at the ocean. Irma was reading to them. He looked at the seascapes again. He and Irma had never suffered any mutual incomprehension when it came to art. In fact, the currents of their imaginations were often in sync.

Back when he was living in San Francisco he had shown her pictures of Christo and Jeanne-Claude's *Running Fence*. She looked at the eighteen-foot veiled white nylon running across the Sonoma hills to the coast and asked to borrow the book. She wanted to show it to her five-year-old students. He looked around at the seascapes again and then out the window at the falling light. Irma was reading *Treasure Island*. Maybe her art was teaching little boys to read. Corny, but that is what he thought.

The next morning, he walked the boys through the high grass and eucalyptus above Manresa State Beach with the Pacific in front of them. He explained slowly that he believed in the individual spirits of all animals and that the wind and rain had spirits too. He said spiritual beings were separate from bodies as immaterial forces that animated the universe. Just knowing that was like praying. And if they believed it, their spirits would ride the wind and the rain across the universe forever.

They asked if that meant they would not have to die.

Ghostbusters

Years later, like a prayer, Nick wrote to him that he often looked to the natural world for comfort, especially when beginning trips of uncertain outcome. He taught that to both of his sons. At least he hoped he had. Irma had given it to him, but somehow without him noticing until he had sons of his own.

They were different little boys than he had been—short-fused and outwardly tough in his way. They had more courage, and more kindness as well. They played Ghostbusters, not World War II and Custer's Last Stand. There were reasons for this, but still . . . Perhaps nothing would serve them better than shaking him off, and he knew that would come. He was already forty-five. Or was it sixty? Long days were turning into short years. One day they would have to make some promises, but not yet.

That made his mind jump. He had always recognized danger, the reality of where and when—and then that bounce of fear. After Beirut, though, he had no longer searched it out. He took his chances, but it was mostly an inner game. His sons were wild in ways he recognized, but also more purposeful, and could be practical almost to hardness. They were like Irma that way when he thought about it. He wanted to put that in a letter to her but could not find the language, and wound up writing that they had *brave hearts*, a vacuousness that embarrassed him.

Nick's passport became thick with added pages. For ten years, he went to wars: Sudan, Darfur, Baghdad, Mosul, Kabul, Helmand, back to Mosul, back to Kabul, Ukraine. Not long after Nick left for Iraq the first time, Thomas left for five months in Ghana with only his phone, the clothes he was wearing, and a small pack of art supplies. Saying goodbye, they joked about Thomas being gang-robbed at knifepoint in Accra, shooting video of the robbers with his phone.

The details of his sons' lives became indelible: a firefight on the road to Lashkar Gah; bad moments scouting film locations around Dadaab; trouble with a former child soldier grabbing at Thomas's long hair . . . Once, waiting for a helicopter back to Kabul, a man with a cigarette asked for a light then leaned in, dropping his head-scarf. The man wanted Nick to see the scarring over his burnt-off face. When Nick told him about that, the humanness of it struck him as unteachable.

He fought off unthinkable thoughts—a bomb vest and a prayer to kill and live forever. A bad checkpoint. Captured. There was nothing as privately terrifying as the idea of a son preparing to die in a way that he, himself, had never been tested. In Bali, Thomas rode a dirt bike, experimented with hallucinogens, and made im-ages of mutant creatures in war paint emerging from a sea littered with plastic bottles. When he heard about that, he thought about his Ducati laid down in a rainy skid, his LSD.

He forgot about inherited weakness and worried about whatever macho inclinations he had passed to them. All the sensitive tough-guy cues, all his stories of courage drawn from dangerous purpose, all that born-to-be-wild, bad-boy poet, smart-jock bullshit . . . He had pushed his sons to play football, starting with official NFL balls left in their cribs. Both surfed and snowboarded. No fear. Combined broken bones: seven before high school. They had all bragged about that. Violent sport as a test of young manhood, full testosterone fervor, never complaining or losing cool, never crying out or regretting or thinking too much.

What if they were out there in the world trying to prove something to him? He could not live with that. They had his approval, no matter what. He would trust Irma's wisdom. They had to make their own lives, their own mistakes, unlinked to any chain of squalid macho. He wished they had spent more time with Irma.

Lakota

Irma was less mysterious now that he had his own sons. She was still patient, but he sensed limits. He also saw how she had encouraged him to respect other people's limits. It was simple, really. Everyone should be allowed to *go their own way*. Most important, Irma told him, *he* should go *his* own way, whichever way that was. He liked that, it was like getting something extra, and his sons liked it even more.

"He goes his own way," he would say about one or the other boy and they would both beam. Sometimes they would say it about each other. He could see it was making them best friends, as well as brothers. That is what he wanted for them.

What the Lakota wanted for their children was that they would walk straight, be polite, and speak softly. He told his sons about this. Also like the Lakota, they would need the audacity to rise to meet whatever came at them. They liked hearing this, and that Irma was interested in the Lakota too. He told them she had given him books about how the Lakota lived, not just how they fought a war with white people to protect their land and who they were.

It was romantic thinking, and he could see how it appealed to them in the way he had liked to play Custer's Last Stand on dirt piles in the orchards he roamed when he was their age. The truth is he was glad Crazy Horse won, although at that age he did not picture Custer naked and white on that hill looking down on the river, with his own bloody penis stuffed in his mouth.

The hell with Custer, anyway. The best part was the continuity of Irma seeing what he was interested in, and encouraging him by being interested herself, and then being the same with her grandsons. It pulled them all together without going to church or even seeing each other very often. When Nick and Thomas asked Irma why she was interested in Indians, she smiled.

"Do not ask why the berries are ripe," Irma said, to give them something to think about, to keep it all going.

Like a Prayer

When he was eight, Irma brought home *Life* magazine with Ernest Hemingway on the cover and *The Old Man and the Sea* inside. Before she read it to him, Irma promised he would like the story, and he did. She knew he was old enough to be moved by the old man, Santiago, dreaming of the lions he had seen playing on an African beach as a young sailor. She wanted him to take that deeper than the words, and told him he could see the lions for himself someday.

From then on, he thought of seeing the lions as a kind of promise from Irma that he could live out whatever he read. Irma encouraged him in this, and by fifth grade, as he read into the Nick Adams stories, he could not keep Bob out of his head. In "Indian Camp," when Nick promises himself he will never be afraid of death, it was like Irma telling him Bob was not afraid to die. Maybe he wanted to come of age, which is what his teachers said the story was about, but he did not care about proving his manhood. Being told he was *the man of the family* had embarrassed him as a little boy, long before he got to Africa, where Ernest had made such a mess.

In Kenya, in ways he could not avoid thinking about, he and his sons were the same as the thousands of trophy hunters who drop into countries suffering lethal poverty to satisfy some archaic manly rite. The difference, of course, between them and Ernest, say, was that they did not kill anything. He thought of Ernest bragging about his lion hunting, and pushing two of his wives to kill lions as well. This disgusted him. He had come to the Maasai Mara to see the animals in their wildness, not as symbols of anything, and he wanted his sons to understand.

It went back to Irma. Her lessons in seeing things for what they were—how to look. Her tree-naming game became a kind of meditation: wooded grassland, circles of acacia—monkey thorn with flowers in long slender spikes, cream to pale yellow. He marked the trees feeding a diversity, from tiny dik-diks to giraffes and elephants. He listened to the birds. Birds everywhere: bateleur eagles, rollers, lappet-faced vultures, bee-eaters, great cormorants, pygmy kingfishers. Ten thousand species from the Nile to the Cape—science overwhelmed. When he had asked Irma her favorite bird, she said all of them. They were looking at the bird book she had given him. He had many favorites—hawks, owls, parrots, one after another. When he told her this, she said it was the same thing with her except she liked them all over and over all the time.

He made early morning game drives, thinking first about the birds, keeping a kind of score with his sightings, but he had no life list. He was not serious in that way, always thinking of other things at the same time. Memories of childhood ricocheted off the hovering of a black-winged kite—Irma telling him to put back the robin's nest with delicate blue eggs he had found in a lilac bush.

When he got out of the Land Rover and walked, there were orange-striped millipedes, fungal termite gardens, beetles that looked like Japanese toys. He went back and picked up one of the beetles. He looked at it. He was *The Walrus*. He remembered his insect collection—what year was that? His pinned tiger monarchs, his *Danaus plexippus*—what grade was he in? His collection was the best in his class. Irma helped him make his killing jar. He had fifty specimens, many moths and butterflies, but also yellow jackets and a dragonfly. He found a black widow exactly where he knew it would be.

When Irma taught him the word *entomology* and what a phylum was, he thought maybe he would be a scientist instead of a fighter pilot. He had not thought about that over all the years, until he was inside a baobab tree on the Zambezi. It felt like a cathedral, Gaudí's Sagrada Família, which reminded him in turn of the Rosicrucian Museum with the shrunken heads.

The first lion he saw was indifferent to the Land Rover, and they got close fast. The richness of the black mane was set off by a tannish brown more golden than he had expected. But it was the size, the four hundred pounds of deep-chested power, that shocked, watching the effortless walk.

He thought about Maasai boys his sons' age hunting lions with spears to prove themselves, to become men on the Maasai Mara. Hemingway's posing was suddenly stupid in a deep, real way, like a dream that jolts you awake, except that he too was now drawn to the lions. The cliché did not bother him. He watched lions rub faces and lean on one another with their tails high, and lick and grunt and snarl and sniff and mark with urine, and purr like the cats they are. None of it was about anyone's manhood.

Lions understood one another, and all the other animals understood them. No spin. No counterspin. Unlike Harvey Weinstein,

144

say, or Bill Cosby or Jeffrey Epstein, and the lengthening line of sexual predators making news back home, lions did not scheme and connive. They had on/off switches triggered by instinct. Nature's interlocking memories, memories of survival . . . They did not send boxes of chocolate penises.

In Hwange, following his friend Julian Brookstein, a third-generation Zimbabwean, they found tracks of many lions crossing a narrow park road. Julian said it was a double pride of twenty-six, with two dominant males, heading toward a mahogany forest rising in the near distance. They reached the mahogany in an hour, and the country opened up with some grassy lots among the trees. Reading tracks in a dry riverbed, they expected to see the pride lying up under some acacia trees maybe one hundred meters beyond where they would climb up the far bank.

If the lions saw them, they could expect lions taking off in all directions, males first. But the lions were not down under the acacia trees, and just over the rise of the bank, the dominant lioness saw them before they saw her. She roared, and the rest of the lions came alive, taking off in different directions, the males out front as Julian had predicted.

When she roared again, two younger lionesses came up on either side of her, but when she charged, she came at them alone, seeming to accelerate. At twenty meters, Julian had his .270 up. He expected a shot, but Julian began shouting, "Hey! Hey! Hey!" and the lioness wheeled off. The younger lionesses followed her, bounding down the hill toward the acacia trees and gone.

The dichotomy between what was dangerous and what was beautiful became no dichotomy at all. The lessons were as simple as

rainy season/dry season. Death from thirst, hunger, exhaustion, pre-
dation. Everything would die. The gazelle fawn frozen, trembling
in the sandy wash, the old buffalo going blind in the tall grass, one
eye already gone. *Waiting*.

At noon the next day, he stood on the airstrip at Giraffe Springs
and felt the heat rising. The lioness and her double pride were
probably just settling down for the afternoon, their instincts in
balance. He and the lioness had crossed paths with no meaning
beyond what had happened. Pay attention, he told himself, you
have no more reason than the lioness to believe the sun will rise
tomorrow.

His motivation to tell this particular story is as complex as weather.
He was drawn toward a reckoning with Ernest when his sons were
born. The so-called Hemingway Code—that sensitive-tough-
guy pose—was his too, and he had gotten it from Ernest. He had
known the stories and the myth, but he had not known that Ernest
started all three of his sons drinking before they were teenagers,
and took Jack, the oldest, to a whorehouse when he was thirteen.
He had not known that on a driven hunt during a school vacation,
Ernest encouraged his younger sons, Gregory and Patrick, to kill
eighty jackrabbits each, and that even as a father he bullied and
seethed and raged on, beating his chest until his boorish and nasty
behavior reflected all the horrors of the manhood he had created
not just for himself but for his sons until he put both barrels in his
mouth and died in his bathrobe.

He remembered Irma reading *The Old Man and the Sea* to him.
Her telling him to make up his own mind had inoculated him. He
despised Ernest now. He had read much about Ernest's problems,

and still he did not care. Ernest's work had fed on his own life until it was ruined, and he was paranoid and depressed and drunk, drunk on himself really.

How fine the dirt, his son Nick thought, as bullets passed overhead in Lashkar Gah, *how blue the sky*. In Shanghai, his son Thomas made bright paintings of street garbage on stretched skins of feral dogs. Would such sons have to die? Yes, and that would be fine, *like a prayer . . . and their spirits would ride the wind and the rain and animate the universe forever.*

3

(COMPENSATION)

He told his assistant he had a plan. When the day came, he would take the express elevator down from the thirty-fourth floor, find his driver, meet his wife at Teterboro, and fly private. Unfortunately, he was not yet sure where they would be going.

She just looked at him.

Preboarding

What passes between a mother and a son is not defined by her love in that moment, but later by the echoes of her motherhood. What did she really do? Her touch. Her courage. No surprise, then, that the more he moved around, changed jobs or just an address, the more he realized how much Irma was still with him.

His adventures in the world, his laughs, his small victories, his own Voyage of Discovery as he had hoped for it when Irma told him about Lewis and Clark and Sacajawea, all reflected Irma's own journey as well as his. He operated out of what she had taught him, a combination of shared instinct and memory. His moves always felt lucky, although Irma would never have gone along with that.

Magazine to magazine, a screenplay here, a new platform there—what was he, anyway, but an aggregation of memories characterized in his various shooting scripts as fast but not loose. Sometimes short, never sweet. Artful only to a point, significant only now, writing this, remembering the falling darkness in his fort and the world's perfection in the tiny scarlet hourglass of a black widow. His childhood. Irma asking what he wanted his life to be.

He could take it easy if he felt like it. He could read more and write and work on his languages. He could travel too, get as far away as he could from whatever assisted-living Place for Dad awaited him. It was easy enough to hide his mounting disappointments. All symptoms, anyway. His self-diagnosis was dizzying. Brilliant friends now mediocre, his own perspicacity fading. People come and go in life, and they came and went in his, most before they passed on any wisdom. He remembered a punch line about never turning down sex or television, but he could not remember the joke.

He was disappointing, balancing on some imaginary tightrope between who he thought he was and who he might actually be. He hoped that was what it meant to be a human being, and that he was not just some guy walking around with a parrot on his shoulder.

His flying dream, he now rationalized, came with the drugs he took to sleep on long-haul flights. Thus the cartoon angle of the descent. Likewise the calm in first class when he looks around and thinks only about the time passing. The metaphor was finally undeniable. Something in his life could end unexpectedly. Was self-doubt undercutting him because his goals were unattainable? What were those goals again?

"Dead Flowers"

Irma asked him once why he wanted to fight about anything that was not his idea. He was a teenager, and this hurt him, but Irma was smiling, teaching. He had no answer. From then on, just remembering her question helped him calm down. Eventually he realized that he had never wanted to fight anybody about anything. He was just afraid of being wrong. When he moved up to a corporate title, Irma's question had gotten him there.

It was not a cowboy movie after all. It was a spy movie—a culture of betrayal. He was a provocateur, a trickster. *To weaponize* was the popular verb, as he praised an outmatched rival to intimidate, or thanked a competitor to sow doubt. *Motherfucker*, he thought to himself. As if to balance such clichés, he worked his way deeper into digital development and tossed references to HTML5 around like Frisbees, although he had never played Frisbee in his life. He forgave himself his jargon because done *was* better than perfect. He said that many times. So-called perfection paralysis was never the problem. It was the inability to start. Sometimes he felt like his little boy self, wandering through childhood interiors, or just sitting uncertainly on the floor of a cheesy tract house in South San Francisco reading about the Pony Express.

Media had become a word that stared back at him pretentiously on his various screens whenever he keyed it in. His finger hovered over the mute button on conference calls. He wanted to bark like Buddy at the end of his chain. Consultants accused one another of trying to *boil the ocean.* Too much *cross-border complexity.* Arf, arf! Everyone was smart and sharp-tongued and wrong about everything. *Juice not worth the squeeze.* Fuck you! But he could not just cock a Colt and step out into the street.

He was fed up. No more braying on conference panels for him. No more picking over greenroom fruit plates. He asked the Human Resources VP what she thought it was about the truth that prevented her from speaking it. At a pitch meeting, he declared the Pony Express his all-time favorite start-up and forewarned the dangers of *HyperNormalisation.* Take that!

He told a brand-wide town hall breakfast that he knew it was going to be a good day because he had heard "Dead Flowers" on Pandora while he was waiting for his black car. He said he owed Keith some kind of royalty. Maybe they should all send Keith a little something.

That night he thought again about Irma driving across Wyoming in her new convertible, top down, hopeful. She would teach school and have a new life without Bob. He wondered how she had gotten the news. A telegram from the War Department? A lieutenant commander at the front door? It must have changed her world in an instant. Did she feel it over and over at different times, shocking her each time?

He had been there too from then on, the two of them driving east and then south and north and, finally, west. She must have had a plan, a secret plan with Norm. She must have thought he had good things for her, for her son—or maybe that son got in their way.

That was Irma's story, where his began. And his story had become the story of the construction of the story of his career—not ironic to anyone but him, living out of balance, backlit with the glare of his ambition. It was time to go. Irma would understand.

Irma

Leaving his office the final time, crossing through the thick, noisy traffic on Fiftieth Street, he saw himself standing around in a dirt hiring lot in Campbell hoping to get picked for a road crew. He remembered the clear light of the early morning, the emptiness of his mind.

Growing up in Campbell, the coolest guys worked construction or in gas stations or as lifeguards. The point was to have a job, not to be the boss, not to run things. Too much hassle. He thought of Irma as a girl, doing her chores, marking time on the family farm, practicing her business letters, writing them out longhand, dreaming of becoming a stenographer.

She had told him she knew she had to get off the farm. But then, of course, there were days now when the farm looked pretty good. The natural world, Bossy the Cow. They laughed a little at that, but just the mention of Bossy the Cow left him with a singular awareness that his days were passing. Irma brought unwanted nostalgia out in him, but he did not get it from her. He was sick of his perpetual regret.

"People come and go," Irma said. "Like you."

"I'm sorry," he said, after a moment.

"No," she said quickly. "I like that."

So did he, and it made him feel lucky again. He finally got it. She had never judged him, and that gave him a freedom he did not appreciate until his sons encroached upon it, at which point he began telling them their first responsibility was to make their lives as interesting as they possibly could. They were just in preschool, but he meant it. *When you live through things, things change you, but you have to keep your life for yourself.* That had been Irma's message, although she never spelled it out in exact words. She had simply taught him to see the trees and the birds.

Taormina

Something was riling him, as if he needed more velocity to catch up with himself—vague, circular reasoning, he knew, but that is how he felt. He needed to get going.

He began traveling compulsively, always with colored pens and a glue stick to fill small journals with notes and whatever he thought to sketch or paste in—museum tickets, stamps, business cards, leaves, feathers. He planned for the journals to become a small library of his eccentricities for his sons to open like time capsules when the moment was right for them, whenever that might be, and to check himself against his own memory.

He had read that memory distills as the years go by, that you wind up with just a single image that is associated with something complicated that was once important to you. That is all you remember because as more and more information fills your brain, you have less control over what you remember. It is harder to find things that remind you of *you*. The journals were supposed to help him with that. He remembered pushing an old John Deere lawn mower back and forth across a neighbor's yard.

Irma's memory was different, of course, like memory is different for everyone. It has to be, and for Irma, the war could not have been the only reverberation, although it was the most obvious. Bob's death had scraped the sides off of her life, streamlined it in a way, although *streamlined* is not a humble enough word. It was a struggle for the right language (*like here*), and then what to do with the sentence once he pulled the words together. It was more like losing Bob had given her something too, made her a straight shooter, honest about whatever she saw (*still not right*).

His most important rule with his journals was that he could not lie to himself, but sometimes he overcorrected. On a trip to Sicily, he brought with him an already bulging journal he had started in Milan, planning to add to it, work it over for a pentimento effect, especially on the page where he had noted his *concerns* regarding how art fit into the passage of time. *Sigh.*

In Taormina, he wandered upon *Teatro antico di Taormina*, a Greek theater from the third century BC that the Romans turned into a colosseum for gladiatorial games. In 132 BC, a slave revolt was suppressed by the Romans and fifteen thousand slaves were thrown off the cliffs of Taormina or crucified in the *teatro*. Now, varied productions were staged there, from opera to rock concerts. Up the hill, the ancient city was overrun by the usual logos— Versace, Prada, Armani, KFC.

He sat under an orange tree at a café table overlooking the site and saw an American family. A man and woman in their early forties were walking in front of a boy and a girl, perhaps seven and nine. The man and woman were bickering and not looking at the ancient theater or paying attention to the children, who watched them closely and stayed close together, knowing what was coming.

When the shouting started, it was sharp and bitter, and he saw the children touch each other for comfort. He had seen his sons do that, and he was suddenly replaying his old arguments with their mother. Then he was following Norm, who was shouting at Irma, and he was terrified of getting left behind at the Santa Clara County Fair. Rage came with that, and guilt, and then what about that time Irma wanted Norm to talk to him about the birds and bees, but not in those words. "Birds and bees" were the words Norm used before he said, ". . . you know, fucking."

He had read enough to know there is no satisfactory science concerning how memories wake up. But they *do* wake up. He knew that too, and what he knew sitting under that orange tree was that, like the slaves who escaped, those two American children would never forget *Teatro Antico di Taormina*.

He opened his journal and began to sketch his brain. He divided the two hemispheres, but not logic juxtaposed to intuition, or math vs. art. He filled both sides full of snakes and bats and tiny dragons swimming toward the center, the longitudinal fissure, flooded with stress hormones. He knew what he meant—trouble at the borders between forgetting and remembering and depression over whatever remained unfulfilled. It ran in families.

Off

He decided to visit all the places he had ever lived. Every house, every apartment. He would *make* photographs. Documentary evidence. It would be an art project, perhaps a book and a show. Variations on his undergraduate appropriations of Joseph Cornell's boxes set down on his specific timeline—a personal atlas of memory.

He made a list: thirty-seven addresses in twenty-six places. Norfolk, Pensacola, Orange, Duluth, Santa Clara, Willow Glen, Burbank, Campbell, Berkeley, San Jose, Newport Beach, Laguna, Los Gatos, Aptos, Madrid, New York, Venice, San Francisco, Denver, Livingston, East Forty-Eighth Street, Bridgehampton, Georgica, Gracie Square, Georgica Association, Amagansett, West Village . . .

He was trying too hard. Mostly he just wanted to refresh his memory. Would that still be art? There was an edge there, he told himself, but it meant nothing beyond the vanity of mythologizing himself. Might as well write a book about staring at the sky.

He visited some of the places anyway, which discouraged him like the occasional bad acid trips he had experienced in his early twenties, before he knew anything about depression. Most of the older addresses were in marginal neighborhoods. The people he saw looked worn and distracted, dispirited by whatever evidence remained to remind of their younger selves.

He remembered odd details from when he had first noticed that some people were a little bit *off*. That was the way Irma would explain herself when something was up but she did not want to talk about it. She would say she was *off*. Or when Calvin Hogg's father came staggering home from the 49er one Saturday night and pulled back the tent flap, leaned his big head in, and said that World War II might have been fine for some people but it sure as hell was not fine for him. Mr. Hogg was drunk, but he was also *off*.

He knew the difference because he himself was occasionally *off*, sometimes *way off*. That was when he remembered that Mr. Hogg had been drinking with Norm that night. How many years ago was that? He knew exactly. He was nine. Norm had called him a pantywaist on his birthday the week before. Where did remembering that lead? What about those toxic proteins building up, forming the plaque that could take him out? What about those spaghetti-like tangles that drop the curtain of Alzheimer's? What if? What if? What if Godzilla comes?

His doctors said he was making himself sick.

Vaccines

He had accumulated many doctors, picking them up over the years as he came down with something or picked up things. He was also preventative, which Irma had explained to him when he got his first flu shot.

He knew it was not just him Irma worried about. She kept up on health developments affecting her students and argued at PTA meetings that their school district should participate in the polio vaccine trials, even though there were press reports that the latest vaccine might cause inflammation of the brain or wear off and leave children in great danger of a more severe type of polio. It was more controversial than flu shots, but Irma did not care.

He knew this at the time because some of his friends told him that was why their parents did not like Irma anymore. He also knew that he had regular checkups and many of those friends only saw a doctor if something was wrong with them or went to the dentist if they got a toothache.

When he told Irma what his friends said, she told him she worried about those kids. She said their parents should "talk to somebody." He did not know what Irma meant. It is probably a function of his selective memory that when it came to mental health he had never been sure how far Irma went beyond being *off* once in a while. He never wondered if Irma was depressed until many years later. He had never even heard her use the word. Now he wondered if Irma had ever felt the past growing around her. That was his symptom.

Screens

Writing in doctor's offices and hospitals killed time.

He was writing about that on his phone, and as he wrote he thought, as he often did, that it was useful the way a single thought could turn into a riff. His mind jumped. A run of waiting memory: babysitting his sister, lying on the floor in front of the TV watching grown-up shows, hearing Norm pull his Cadillac into the driveway, Irma checking on him pretending to be asleep in his bed until she closed the door, reading under the covers with his flashlight. He turned that over and waited for the needlegrass sprouting tall and green from the damp, black soil, and there he was, suddenly and yet again, sitting in his fort in the field behind the house on Settle Street in Willow Glen, thinking about time passing.

He made a note.

Waiting. Waiting then, waiting now, in a waiting room at Lenox Hill anticipating CAT-scan results. Lenox Hill was familiar in a bad way. Not efficient, not well-run, tired. His expensive doctor was not on top of this, did not prepare him. He thought about Thomas, with his lungs collapsing. He wondered again if Thomas could remember. If that was what made him brave.

More waiting. He was resigned.

He could feel his blood pumping. Some unsteadiness, but not dizzy. No bounce of fear. Noted. And now he was thinking about his sons' courage, his own bravery probably just a fear of failure. Not tough but not afraid to fight. Come fast and hard . . . Where did he learn that? Not from Irma. But there he was, every time, fast and hard.

Nick had told him that when he was a young correspondent embedded with the 1st Cavalry in Mosul a sergeant asked him if it was his first experience of combat and Nick said, Nah, he had been in something in Darfur, which was not quite true. And yet he could easily conceive the scenario, the Janjaweed rounds ripping the wadi at carotid height, strongly and instantly zipping past, then the horses . . . Nick could see it clearly the instant he lied to the sergeant. He did not think the sergeant believed him, but it did not matter. They were sitting on the edge of cots in a two-man hooch where a rocket landed a week later but did not detonate.

He made another note.

What was more vivid to Nick, what was *real*, was the subway gray of the sky in Mosul where he first took fire.

Another note.

Some notes he saved. It was a kind of exercise, like looking things up, writing things down, like Irma had taught him. Black widows like all spiders, he learned, were *Iktomi* to the Lakota, trickster-healers in cahoots with the *Heyoka*, spirits taller than their shadows, thunder dreamers, contrary warrior clowns, crazy in a sacred way. Crazy Horse was *Heyoka* when he rubbed out Custer.

Deep breath. He felt pretty good, actually.

Post-Traumatic

He walked the city thinking that not counting his steps anymore was progress. He quoted Irma to himself about how *small things can mean a little too much*. Just knowing this could wear you down, thinking too hard about it could crush you. No need to put crosshairs on your own chest. Nice try.

There were many trees in his neighborhood in Greenwich Village, but mostly elms and maples. The only birds he saw were sparrows and pigeons, with occasional gulls over the river, not birds for him now so much as the idea of birds. Sometimes the idea of things would have to be enough. He hated that.

At his yearly physical, he told his longtime doctor he was not sleeping well.

"For how long?" the doctor asked.

An obvious question, and he wondered to himself why he had never mentioned it. That was funny. "My whole life," he said.

"Well, then . . ." the doctor suggested he see *someone*, specifically a psychopharmacologist, but offered only a flimsy definition of what he was suffering. Depression, sure, but how was that different from a *normal* reaction of a *normal* human facing a *normal* circumstance—growing old? How *off* was that? What would the drugs make better? His desolate melancholy? What a wimp. His glum, ferocious anger? What a bully. His sadness for no reason? What a crybaby. Post-traumatic stress disorders from childhood still unprocessed? That babysitter? Lying awake in his bed, not knowing that he was waiting, unconsciously, for Norm to come home drunk?

He told the doctor he would think about it. Right, he thought to himself, think about it. He remembered Irma going over his report cards with him at the kitchen table, him saying he never interrupted his teachers, her telling him to think a little harder about that.

Think

Think, think, think. What if he was thinking too much, thinking a little more about too many things. So what? Thinking was just selective memory anyway. Put two things together that have never been together before, and the world is changed. *Chaos theory.* Memory works that way too. No story is told just once, but it is never exactly the same story . . . That was all he needed to know, except certain memories seemed to be searching him out, and since the brain handles positive and negative information differently, in different hemispheres, troubling info, what most people don't want to think about, takes more time to process, which means more thinking, and bad events are harder to forget and wear off more slowly, some never.

But you can bury them. He was aware.

Piece of cake.

When he finally told Irma about Norm running his Cadillac off the road, he did not tell her about lying to the policeman. He did not want to disappoint her, but she saw through him and said she knew he was thinking about too many things at once. That was not how she said it.

"You've got a lot on your mind" is what she said. That was how she let him off.

Now he needed to let himself off. He was nervous in ways he did not recognize. This was unexpected and troubling, but he was still himself too, so he began making a plan, many plans. Work was never just work for him. It had to be more, which he now saw was what Irma was getting at when she was still substituting and told him she hoped that when he grew up his job would be different every day like hers was. That was the thing about teaching.

Irma was such a popular teacher that the customary elementary school Christmas gifts—meant to be modest and thoughtful but fun like a light scarf or a box of Christmas candy—left her finally with way too many of the cute salt-and-pepper-shaker sets that Mrs. Elden was said to collect. How this started was mysterious to her, but every few years she drove to Gilroy so that she could donate a couple boxes of them to a thrift shop without fear of being found out by bargain-hunting PTA mothers.

Irma did not know how to end the cycle without hurting feelings. It was not lying except perhaps by omission. The irony, of course, was that after only five years Irma wound up with an impressive collection of black and white Scotty dogs—the only ones she saved. They reminded him of the Scotty dog he liked at that first motel on the El Camino.

So perhaps he would teach. Irma taught for fifty years and her values could become his values. She taught reading. He would have to teach journalism. Journalism was about finding out, not already knowing, but when he thought harder about teaching, it was not the skills and ethics that came to him but the grinding, corporate business of it.

He did not want to lecture on cost-cutting. The relentlessness of it had taught him about the humiliation of the inevitable, or was it dignity when aged-out colleagues told him they were sorry he had to deliver such terrible news? That would not be teaching any more than it had been editing. Irma would understand.

Perhaps he was not fit to teach anyway. Certainly there were no teaching vacancies appropriate for him to fill, although journalists he knew as rivals were sitting in prestigious chairs at fine universities. Many more writers and editors who had worked for him were scratching around in academia as adjunct professors. So how about a seminar on crypto-genderism and new media? Fine with him.

His bitterness troubled him. It was embarrassing and small, like this little rhetorical trick of bringing up something while denying that it should be brought up. He had read about that somewhere. *Apophasis*. So yes, whatever, he just wanted the status.

That was all over anyway. He worked for himself as a writer, after all, and as a consultant or digital developer or whatever, depending on the meeting. Sometimes he felt like a little boy showing off, waiting for Irma to tell him to settle down.

Treadmill

Working out at his gym he read on his phone that the endlessness of filling orders for Amazon (or whatever) was a long heave from any time-warp extension of carrying water. This was so smart it intimidated him as he walked home from the gym, counting his steps again, thinking about all the words he had written over his life and what they amounted to.

When his novel had finally come out, one reviewer praised "the madness, the unhinged Golden State euphoric/utopian visions, the violence lurking under the Didion-esque (Hockney-esque?) sunlight." The language in that review was sharper than his own words in the novel. He saw connections, not patterns exactly but something about seeing David Hockney strolling around campus in his polka-dot suit and then, years later, being described as Hockney-esque.

It was also a close description of his state of mind as a teenager. Fitting then that he had dedicated the novel to Irma: "For my mother who as far as I know invented artichokes." That was a surprise for her. She thanked him with one of her formal notes, writing simply that she was proud of him. He had not heard that from her since he was a little boy.

Movie Dreams

Maybe he would write another novel. Make up a story to sneak up on what it was like to be alive. He was not thinking about what technology and media were doing to people's brains, or the squeezing depression and anger of poverty everywhere in the world. That was pretentious, too *highfalutin*, as Irma would say. He just wanted to point out a couple of things and avoid infestation, maybe expose something real of the life he was now peeling back. He thought more and more about Irma. How she would tell him to use his imagination. She had been serious.

He identified with writers who planted themselves in the natural world, although he could bullshit easily with writers who were praised for living in the world of ideas. Either way, he was looking for ways his ideas might make it to the page, the sacred page where he learned to think as he had learned to read, with wonder, the way Irma had taught him. Like water flowing over stones, his mind ran with new intention to write, maybe even about Irma. He closed his eyes and saw her talking a highway patrolman out of a speeding ticket.

IRMA

He thought again about how he was going to fuck Norm's cute girl-friend. He had put that away long ago with a sickening feeling. Now he imagined his unconscious dragging it out like a lost glove that needed to be paired or thrown away. If he was going to write about Irma, he needed to shake all the trees and look closely at whatever fell out.

Shake the trees? Old gloves? He winced at the tropes. He would simply write about Irma, not a mission statement, something simple to be read in a single sitting about how before he could remember anything else he remembered her teaching him the names of things. That was her alchemy, and somehow it had given him an idea of what the fuck to do with the bitterness of washing her vomit off Norm's Cadillac.

A feeling welled up. Writing about Irma was profane, then quickly it was like a barely flickering dream that dissipates as soon as you wake up. He remembered Irma telling him that dreams were good, that he should never be afraid of them because they were always telling him something. That was why he should try to remember them and think about them. It was good for him to have little movies in his head.

When he was older, he knew she was not talking about self-important dreams like his airliner going down. Dreams like that followed him into the day and seemed to be crying out for interpretation when he did not want to think about any of it. He liked movies in his head anyway. He let his mind run:

OPEN-ON: Wyoming. Night. A pretty woman with a small child in a convertible speeds into the darkness. A motel erupts in flames in the rearview mirror . . .

Or better:

DISSOLVE TO: Cheyenne dog soldiers appear on a rise above a solitary cabin at a bend in a river. A handsome woman and a little boy in the ranch yard look up . . .

The Hamilton Lounge

When he started writing again he was alone all day, every day. Some days he did not speak at all. He sat at his screen, hoping to find precise language about real people doing real things, stories with meaning beneath the surface of the words that showed dignity and even glamor in exactly that—*real life*. So he was writing about himself writing on his screens. Readers would understand and see he made a point of going no further than he went. That was the point. That would be the art.

He thought of his process as ruthless, also hilarious. He welcomed selfish distractions. By six p.m., he needed to change his point of view. He had a drink. Maybe it was all about drinking anyway. Irma had been right. Drinking was expensive, but in ways he had not understood, even as an adult when he thought he knew exactly what she had meant.

There was a bar called the Hamilton Lounge in a new shopping center that went up less than a mile from Irma's house after he was gone. Sometimes Irma went there with the other teachers after school on Fridays. He knew this because he had seen her car in the parking lot. Irma drove a Volkswagen for a while and then bought a new Pontiac, a "palomino copper" two-door Bonneville, which she said she bought because she felt like getting around a little more. It was the Bonneville he saw parked at the Hamilton Lounge.

Irma told him she did not like bars, but the Hamilton Lounge was different because there were no drunks, and sometimes teachers liked to get together without kids around, maybe let their hair down a little. Sometimes she met other interesting people. One of the times he thought to call her to check in, he teased that he might drop by the Hamilton Lounge some Friday and buy her a drink.

"Don't you dare," Irma said quickly.

After that he began to notice other cars parked at the Hamilton Lounge, often the Jeep used by the father of his friend from Patch Ave to drive between his various jobs as a paving contractor. So he never went to the Hamilton Lounge. But now, after a million drinks after work, after breaking into houses to steal liquor, after what that first maraschino cherry tasted like, after offering highballs to Pops's pals, he was back to having more drinks after work. And where was that joint? That half gram? That black tab with the white dot?

Maybe he would start getting high again.

Time to Destination

What is easy to see now that was impossible for him to see then is that there was a stretch of time when Irma did not think about him nearly as often as he thought about her. She was concentrating on her real estate and not traveling again yet, but told him she appreciated a call whenever he was leaving or just back. When he told her about his trips, even her slight interest felt like validation that he might actually be learning something. Exactly what he wanted to see in *his* sons.

It seemed to please her that he kept a running count of countries in order of first visited—seventy-three—but they both knew his list was more about his own vanity than useful inventory for her. He sometimes returned to the same places, hoping for the best, checking in and out of progressively better hotel rooms in Athens, Beijing, Delhi. All the same room, really, ambered by luxury and security. Ever-higher thread counts, malachite bathrooms, minibars like vaults protecting tiny whiskey bottles and packages of M&M's like artifacts. He told Irma every room was a civilizing cave, but sadly no sympathetic magic. No mastodons scratched on the walls, outlined in a paste of blood and root.

Irma liked hearing the contents of the different minibars, but told him it was not something he should talk about with what she called his new *show-off language.* Before he could question what she was talking about, Irma told him she was still his mother. To tease her, he described the netherworld of BA's Concorde Room at LHR, Cathay Pacific's The Pier in HKG, Qatar Airways' Al Safwa Lounge at DOH, like a museum, the ceilings forty feet tall. He said just knowing the names was a kind of currency. Irma was unimpressed. She told him she could not imagine how preboarding could be a reason to travel.

He looked at old people and saw their younger faces. On planes, this was calming but sad, especially flying long-haul out of JFK. Cabin attendants with million-mile smiles. Time to destination.

On American to Lima, he swallowed a pill, stared into his vodka, and started counting down to his flying dream—predictable now. The vodka tasted slick, like the facilitator it is. He read an interview in the *TBR* with Eve Ensler, a writer and playwright of reputation he had never met. Eve wrote, "I was a deeply traumatized child." He wondered what *deeply* meant.

Eve said, "Stories of war, climate disaster, immigration abuse, racism, violence against women often inhabit my dreams." He wondered what those dreams looked like. Eve dreamed a lot: "I dream of books seeping into me through osmosis and I am strengthened to feel part of a continuum and community of writers." He knew Eve was making a point. He wished, without smirking, that he could have that dream.

He knew from a guidebook that they drank in ancient Peru, often to drunkenness, as evidence of piety and to talk to their gods. Whatever. He did not know why he was sitting there with his seat belt fastened, only that he was some kind of serial pilgrim, which left him with an overriding sense of the transience of everything—places, people, circumstance. He remembered Irma driving with the top down, making him giggle, singing along to the radio. Why not? he thought, and committed to an existential view of his trip. He was going to Peru because he was going to Peru—even the dreaded Machu Picchu. Irma had hated Machu Picchu.

When Irma and Carl had begun to travel out of boredom with retirement, she set all the itineraries. If she wanted to go marlin fishing out of La Paz, they went marlin fishing out of La Paz. She told Carl, who did not fish, that she had fished with her family as a girl and always loved fishing. She sent him a photo of herself and Carl standing on a dock with a huge blue marlin hanging between them. He had a similar photo of himself on the same dock in his early twenties showing off a marlin he had caught when Hemingway was still baiting him.

After Irma spent a month in New Zealand, she described it to him as California a hundred years ago. You should go there, she told him. She and Carl might even move there. He meant to do that, get to New Zealand, but now he was simply where he was, on his way to fucking Machu Picchu.

To save himself he would look for small truths. Irma had always told him it was admirable to want to learn what she called *the whole wide world*, but he should try to know some small truths too. He thought of a barefoot and pregnant girl he had seen on one of his many trips to Mexico. Almost a child, really. She was sweeping a dirt yard next to a gas station in Chihuahua, where many of the children Irma taught to read were from.

Linkage was important. Birds flushed out of his memory. A burrowing owl on a ranch road in New Mexico. Bald eagles fishing the Yellowstone behind his house in Montana. The pair of peregrine falcons nesting on a window ledge of the Metropolitan Life Building in Manhattan. All of them Irma's favorite.

He had a knot on his stomach where he and Irma had been connected, and he was more connected now than he knew. It was an extraordinary thing.

Wednesday Meetings

Back in New York he felt lighter, also tougher. But jumpy.

What was he afraid of? Not aging or death. Derangement, maybe, running wild through his own memory. Pulling that thread, he found a therapist close to his age in the West Village. He thought it would be important not to have to explain Vietnam.

At their first meeting, the therapist asked about his childhood, if he had been a happy little boy. An obvious question, but he had not anticipated it. He said he was raised by his mother. The therapist suggested that mothers and sons are one thing, but single mothers and fatherless sons are something else entirely. Such sons tend toward violence, for one thing. Did he love his mother? Did they have a hard time? Was there enough money?

When he did not answer immediately, the therapist leaned back in his chair and explained that poverty-induced stress can change the frontal cortex of a child before he is five years old. Changes the way the child thinks.

They were never poor, he told the therapist, but it was complicated because he had an asshole for a stepfather for a while. Ten years.

What about violence, the therapist asked, or any kind of abuse?

He said he knew where the therapist was going, and no, he had never felt like a victim. Plus, he went on, Oedipus may have killed his father and married his mother, but Freud ignored the part of the myth in which Oedipus's father, Laius, crippled Oedipus as a child and exposed him in the wilderness to die.

The therapist said he was pleased to have a new patient who was interested in Freud.

After that first meeting, the therapist talked a lot, sometimes more than he did. He had not expected this, and was grateful. The therapist talked about Freud's "Wednesday Meetings" with a small circle of his colleagues and supporters, during which complex discussions of case histories were finished off with a summary by the great man. Some of the members presented detailed histories of their own psychological and sexual development. "Risky business," the therapist said.

His appointments were also on Wednesdays, which was too corny for either of them to mention, but they soon developed insignificant bonds over celebrities they both knew, with implications that the therapist was treating them. For what? The usual.

Once a week that spring, he would walk across Greenwich Village to a high-rise condo off Washington Square where the therapist kept a penthouse office. The therapist asked him if he understood that his unconscious was working overtime to defend against anxiety by burying painful feelings or thoughts. Sure he did.

The therapist explained, as if talking to a child, that repression is the basis for all other defense mechanisms *and* bad behavior on the road to debilitating depression. The implication was that he had to unmask himself. He wrote that down on his phone. The therapist liked it when he did that—wrote something down.

His sessions came to be explorations of those defense mechanisms. The first and most obvious was his in-and-out memory, how much he blocked. Was it possible to put something behind you if you could not remember it in the first place? He could see Irma on her knees, with Norm standing over her. That image had never left him, but what else was there? What about people whose lives touched him only briefly but that he remembered with guilt as significant loss? He barely knew anything about Clydia, except that she had looked like Natalie Wood and lived in a foster home and he should have helped her. The therapist wanted more, but that was all he had.

The therapist was also interested in his flying dreams. He still had them, but now sometimes they came with a sense of approaching freedom, almost euphoria. It was like he was avoiding a close call, or was about to win something—not a prize, more like getting away with something. The therapist insisted on Freud's theory of flying dreams as sexual relief.

Fine, but still, why the sensation of waiting and waiting . . . ?

"You tell me," said the therapist, smiling with slyness.

He and the therapist agreed he was not normal. He was high-functioning, yes, but too repressive, too regressive, and he was a bad sublimator. Well, fine, but he wanted to bring it all back to his *untimely demise*. Back to terror management theory, mortality salience and all that. Good. The therapist's interest in death, focused on how various people coped with "advancing horizons."

Nope.

He was a different story. For him, it wasn't aging. Shriveled like a monkey was fine with him. The therapist crossed his arms over his chest and said the suicide rate among men their age had jumped 45 percent since 1999. As if, he thought, even though you never know. Close friends had killed themselves. He had thought about their last moments, the final secret they kept as they reached for the pills or loaded the .45.

"Tell me about *that*," said the therapist, looking concerned.

Zoo

He walked down Madison Avenue, which always reminded him of his sons because of the proximity to their school. They loved their school, but not like he had loved his easy grades and his football. They played football, and their grades were good, but they did not need to be the smartest in the class. He had wanted to be the smartest, no matter what.

Irma did not believe in IQ tests. She gave them to her students as part of required academic tracking but knew they favored children with early reading exposure, like him. She would sometimes bring tests home and let him look. He liked taking them, as if proving a point he wanted desperately to prove but did not yet understand.

"You're smart enough," Irma would say when he asked for his score.

"What number?" he would always press.

"Slightly above average."

If this threw him into a pout, as it usually did, she would ask him if he had learned anything that day. What had he connected in that crazy head of his? That was the way to be smart.

He stopped at St. James' Church. It was empty except for a young guy in a dirty hoodie asleep in one of the back pews. He slid in behind the kid, who had his head on the middle aisle armrest as if having fallen asleep leaning to look at the ass of a girl he used to fuck walking up the aisle to marry a rich guy. Where did that come from?

No clue.

He tried to remember his lowest day, but maybe that would be his last day—by definition. Or his last day would be his best—also by definition. There was an incalculable number of shadings in such inventories—annoying like offstage noise.

The church was quiet. The kid looked surprisingly young, with his shoes off, a small, tattered backpack and a bulging garbage bag at his bare feet. He wondered where he was from, closed his eyes and saw him hitchhiking on a back road out of some nameless town, never coming back.

Scandy came back to him, along with Fronie's deer rifle. He slipped a $20 into the kid's backpack and walked to the Central Park Zoo.

Reunion

He heard from a high school classmate he did not remember. She was glad she found him. There was going to be a reunion. There had been many reunions, but he was hard to find if you still lived in Burbank or Campbell or Willow Glen or wherever she lived. She sent a list of classmates and what they were up to after fifty years. Clydia was dead, gone at twenty-seven, June 16, 1971. It did not say how she died. In June 1971, thirty, or whatever, years ago, he was in Italy with Nadine. Or maybe it was Greece. He hoped Nadine was not dead.

His plane was late into SFO. By the time he got to the reunion at an Italian restaurant down the peninsula, almost everyone was gone or leaving. His old friend, the good athlete from Patch Avenue, was still there, and so was a popular girl they both had liked. His friend had played basketball at a small college in the Midwest and then stepped into his father's paving business. You could still see the grace in the way he carried himself, and the girl had that too—her knowingness, maybe.

They were glad to see each other, but there was no spark. They were not with anyone, but they did not want each other anymore.

He remembered that Irma had seen his friend's father a couple of times after Norm was gone. Not just at the Hamilton Lounge. He was not supposed to know that. He wondered if his friend knew. It was another secret, a tiny wave in an ocean of secrecy—people giving up, people starting over.

When his friend and the girl left in different directions, he drank with the stragglers. No one he had been close to, but they were fine, not obviously sad or diminished, but older, he thought, than what he saw in his mirror. They thought he was still a journalist. He said he was in California to see the fires, which was half true. They talked mostly about who was rich or dead. He asked if they knew where the last orchard was.

They said they were glad he was still ironic.

The next morning, he drove around. It was late March, the kind of bright Saturday that would have seen him out early on his Phantom. His old streets were wider than he remembered, with mature trees now, thick black oaks and walnuts grown tall. No more vacant lots. He parked across from the house on Bradley Avenue and took an iPhone shot to send to his sons. It was well-kept, with a small, neat lawn, but the house next door was run-down, cement where the lawn had been, where he had sat pulling up grass with Gerald, waiting to see if Margo was going to be okay.

He went to his phone again to see what had happened to Gerald. The family's carpet store was now a privately held corporation with commercial flooring contracts in excess of $1 billion. It was incorporated in 1954, the same year Margo got that line drive in the face. There was a photo of Gerald as CEO, with three of his executives. He looked trim, with silver hair and expensive clothes.

He tried Clydia. Nothing. He tried Irma Sophronia Nelson Mc-Donell Elden Edwards. Nothing. He tried himself. Too much.

He opened the car door to get a wider view of the house, but could not frame what he had come for.

Back up the San Francisco peninsula, with the Santa Cruz Mountains to the west. The subdivisions and shopping centers and strip malls and convenience stores and fast-food drive-throughs had spread everywhere. Irma's Valley of Heart's Delight was gone.

The apricots and cherries came from Mexico now, the almonds and walnuts from Vietnam. He kept driving: Santa Clara (prunes/Intel), Sunnyvale (apricots, almonds/Yahoo), Mountain View (peaches, strawberries/Google), Cupertino (cherries, sweet corn/Apple), Los Altos . . . Nick had been to Los Altos to interview the parents of a young marine captain killed in a green-on-blue attack at a Special Operations base in Helmand. He could read Nick's book back in his hotel room. If he felt like it, he could listen to Nick reading it on his iPhone. It was all connected.

The most attractive side of Steve Jobs was how sentimental he got when he talked about Cupertino, his "Valley of the Heart's Delight," where he had dropped acid in the blooming fields. Steve talked about it all the time, even when the orchards were gone. Before Apple, when he lived in the Santa Cruz Mountains, people said he was a hippie. Programmers, engineers, HR VPs lived in those mountains now. The summer cabins on Ogallala Warpath were redone in minimalist design. Chemeketa Park was six miles from Netflix headquarters in Los Gatos, two blocks from where Virginia Darnay lived that year she taught high school French.

Duluth

The therapist died on a weekend vacation to St. Barths. The previous Wednesday they had discussed death as usual, but it had not gone well. Perhaps they were both a little *off*. The therapist asked him how it was going with his drinking. He asked the therapist what it felt like after fifty years of ineffective and remunerative speculation on the work of a single artist, Anna Freud, to have so profoundly and pathetically missed the point. Did it feel like dog-paddling?

He felt bad immediately. The therapist looked as if he might cry.

Maybe the therapist was in love with him.

Why would he think such a thing? Why was he so angry?

The therapist told him that his manly plumage and smart-jock posturing was still covering something. Or maybe, he suggested back to the therapist, it had something to do with the weather, like the prairie madness that comes on the winds across the northern plains. The therapist insisted that that too was his masculinity fucking with him again.

When he was seven, before his sister was born, Irma and Norm had taken him back to Duluth for Christmas. They were going to visit

Nana and Pops and Uncle Jack. He did not remember Nana except for her taking his cowboy boots. Irma told him Nana had sent small presents for him to open along the trip so he would not be bored. Irma said Nana loved him the same way she had loved Bob. He should love his Nana back. They were going to visit Fronie and his Grandpa too, if it was not too cold. There would be lots of snow out on the farm.

The morning they left was the second day of the worst storm on record in the Santa Clara Valley. They took a cab through blowing rain to the Southern Pacific Depot in San Jose and then spent three days on a train. He got to open his first present passing through Sacramento. It was a toy soldier throwing a grenade. Climbing into the Sierras, he opened another, a rifleman shooting from a knee. The train was hot and stuffy. He held his men and pressed his face against the cool windows. It was hard to see outside. Irma said they were going back the same way they had driven to California, except it was faster on the train. Out his window, the wind swept the dark prairie.

In Minneapolis, they got on a Greyhound bus. When they arrived in Duluth, it was dark and snowing in swirls illuminated by the bus lights. He had six new army men.

When they got off the bus, his grandpa was waiting. "Mrs. McDonell died last night," he said to Irma. That was his nana who was dead now. His grandpa then turned, looking down to him. "That's why your pops isn't here."

He was afraid he might cry. Irma reached down and hugged him to her.

Pepsi Road

He counted on his brain to throw light on things, his own personal blinding light, blinding to him anyway. And in his walking trances, a sense of whirling somehow watching himself from above, seeing his life spooling out into time and reeling back out of sequence, never quite snapping into place.

He walked two miles up the Hudson to the USS *Intrepid*. The old carrier had survived kamikaze attacks and torpedo strikes fighting the Japanese fleet in the Pacific. Then moonshot recovery and Vietnam. It was now a museum that he had avoided all his years in New York for reasons he had never identified. He was kidding himself.

On the flight deck he inspected a Grumman TBM-3E Avenger from 1942 with .50 caliber wing-mounted machine guns, triggering an image of a tombstone in that cemetery in Duluth, where he stood beside Irma and watched his nana lowered into the ground. There was an airplane chiseled into the stone and some words he could not read.

He walked home the long way, crossing the busiest streets against the lights. His anger was not a surprise. He was not the first writer to wonder if it was worth it, another experiment in recovered memory in search of what? He remembered the cap pistol he had wanted as a child.

He kept walking.

Nick walked the devastated streets of Mosul, *devastated* a meaningless word. Nick emailed from Pepsi Road, the front line. The stink of bodies fouled the cool night air. There was mortar fire. A father rushed from the bombarded ISIS side over the line to an Iraqi Special Ops position. He was carrying a small boy in his arms. The father, in shock, thought his son was alive. No, the soldiers said, the boy was dead. The man began to wail. He had two sons, twins. The air strike had killed one of them, and he'd decided to try to escape with the other. *Inshallah*. He quickly dug a shallow grave, the closest he could come to halal burial, laid the dead son down, and covered him. Then he scooped up his other son and ran. But in his panic he had taken the dead boy and buried the living one.

The Long Now

He stared out over the Hudson River looking for a grip. A waste of time, he knew. The view was too familiar—*his* view from *his* desk in *his* studio in *his* building on *his* street in *his* neighborhood in *his* city. Dreary rounds of errands. *What did he want his life to be?* There were no clues across the river in New Jersey, only the banality of second-string skyscrapers. He thought of Irma, and wondered what she might have seen.

Those fissures were still on his mind. He went to his journals and looked at his brain drawings. There were more of them now, but all hitting his predictable bumpers—all variations on chemical mash-ups of memory and depression. Big fucking trouble, unfulfilled dreams. Courage and character were supposed to matter, and he would never believe it (the slide) was inevitable.

He needed information, insights: how his own life braided out of Irma's. To be self-aware, like Irma, he had to see things for what they were. That was Irma in spades, her echoing wisdom. The natural world, turning over every fraction of every fraction of every second. Evolution on the Clock of the Long Now. The meaning of humanness.

Art

The *idea* of art came roaring back at him. What was it with him as an artist, anyway? Well, maybe he just wanted to be different, and artists were different. The narcissism of that was deadening.

He remembered signing over the rights to his *747* photographs to Chris Burden in that booth at the Hinano Cafe. Burden had matured into an installation artist whose models and kinetic sculptures hit him like mesmerizing toys. Burden's rows of obsolete streetlights rewired for solar illuminated the Los Angeles County Museum like a Forest of Light—art as collective memory—a masterpiece.

So where was *his* masterpiece? Maybe you had to be able to draw that white bowl of hard-boiled eggs after all. That was obvious once you got a clue—like seeing Burden's beautiful drawings of imagined machines. All he knew now was that an hour spent every day at the Met or MoMA or the Guggenheim helped him think— put two and two together, as Irma would say.

He wandered the high-ceilinged galleries with no destination except *to see what he would see.* All three museums had pieces by Burden in their permanent collections. All the minimalists he had known at Irvine were there as well. He looked up a John Baldessari lithograph he remembered, done the same year as *747.* It was titled

I Will Not Make Any More Boring Art, and repeated that sentence seventeen times in longhand, filling a page of typing paper, mocking conceptual art even as it stood as a definitive example.

The handwriting looked like his, another tangled knot he needed to loosen. Just because he understood something did not make it his idea too. Irma always told him not to take credit, never. If something was truly his, everyone would give him credit soon enough. He was not sure about that.

To relieve himself from this false weight, he surveyed the museums' collections from ancient civilizations and landed on Carthage. The Phoenicians had interested him as a boy, their sophisticated navigation, Hannibal and his war elephants in the Alps. In Gallery 171 at the Met, he found tiny glass heads honoring the Phoenician deities of Carthage—the goddess Tanit and her consort Baal. The heads were unbalanced and fish-eyed, demented in a way that would stay with him, like the baby heads in the Rosicrucian Museum in San Jose.

Researching his renewed interest online, he read that Carthaginians ritually sacrificed their children. He was still seeing those tiny glass heads of princess Tanit and the murderous Baal, and he had more questions. He had answered his shrunken-head questions at the Pitt Rivers Museum at Oxford, standing in front of a glass case labeled *The Treatment of Dead Enemies*. Those heads in the Rosicrucian Museum were not the heads of children. That was important, directional in some way.

So he would go to Carthage. Look directly at its atrocity. See things for what they were, remember what he needed to remember, learn what he needed to learn. Find his own truth in what bothered him. He would listen for echoes. Maybe he could be an artist after all.

Carthage

The Tophet of Carthage was ten kilometers from The Four Seasons Tunis, in the affluent suburb of Gammarth. Some of the earliest gravesites were in small groups surrounded by daily life—an old woman feeding chickens, a shop selling SIM cards. The archeology was complicated, precise. Ancient texts and archeological digs mapped young children and infants interred in small vaults with amulets, and sometimes kittens. Or the children were ashes, Tophet from the Hebrew *topheth*, derived from "drum" or "place of burning," an open area for sacrifice.

He walked among the many graves dedicated to Tanit, expressed as Tanit's symbol, a disc balanced on a line across the apex of a pyramid. The line had upturned ends, a child with outstretched arms. Later, he came to a firepit in that shape with metal grates to lower the children. What was asked for in return—what favors, what forgiveness? What was granted?

He sat on the ground and read the Roman Diodorus Siculus's 310 BC description of the sacrifice of children by parents who had vowed to offer their next child if the gods would favor them: if their shipment of goods—the textiles, the glass, the slaves—were to arrive safely in a foreign port. The rich Carthaginians placed their children in the arms of a bronze statue of Tanit . . . *The hands of the statue extended over a brazier into which the child fell once the flames had caused the limbs to contract and its mouth to open . . . The child was alive and conscious when burned . . . The sacrificed child was best-loved or more often a poor child purchased as a substitute . . . If there were too many children their throats were cut as if so many lambs or young birds . . .*

That was enough. His quest, taken up on a whim, was now an unbearable reality. There were no adult graves at the Tophet of Carthage. Unthinkable narratives. He turned off his phone. His ignorance was infinite, his compassion strangely bitter. Still no satisfactory definition of collateral damage, no official empathy for families walking north, detained, children separated, white supremacists strutting their stuff, active shooters. Nothing surprised him. The worst of times, he thought, but they were not.

Not even close . . .

4

(RETREAT)

Something was coming. It was growing around him, distraction mostly, but fretful. He is asking you to stay with him, to stay with Irma. It takes a long time to tell the truth, something else they both believed but never said.

Dawn Patrol

Cold, hard rain blew off the Hudson with the smell of stone from the bulkheads. New York was locking down. He saw the galloping death count on his screens and remembered Irma and Norm arguing about flu shots. That dead girl in Willow Glen. Norm had said not to be so sure it was the flu, or that some girl they did not even know was really dead. So what if it was in the paper! Irma asked Norm why anyone would lie about the death of a little girl. It was not a question.

They had sent him to the backyard. He remembered Irma framed by the kitchen window. She was infuriated, standing up to Norm, holding her ground. There would be a lesson in that argument. He could sense it coming.

The morning after the case count tripled, he drove through the city with the sun coming up, as he had done with his sons when they were little. On Sundays, he would get them up and dressed in the dark and into the black Suburban he had then. They would stop at the all-night diner on Eighty-Ninth Street for his coffee and croissants and juice for them. Then they would drive the city—up into Harlem on First Ave, then across Martin Luther King Boulevard at the top of Central Park, and left down Broadway—taking time to see whatever they would see as the light came up. It was the same game Irma had played with him in Willow Glen. He would hear the phone ring early, and she would come to his bed and tell him she was going to substitute again.

"Dawn patrol," Irma would say. "Let's see what we can see."

She would drive slowly to his school, and he would watch carefully out the window. Irma told him learning how to look was more important than what he saw—men in overalls going to construction jobs, robins pecking lawns for worms. Time would speed up until she dropped him off. Then he would sit on a playground bench and watch the older kids and wait.

He was in a new Suburban now, another black one, unusual for a rental. The clean smell suggested well-being, but he had been self-quarantined for two weeks. The days had overlapped. He went out only to walk the dog. People he saw avoided eye contact with resignation, hints of coming despair.

There were many stories about the frontline health workers, how brave they were. Stories built on stories. Black, Latino, lower-income families three times as vulnerable. Shameful inequities everywhere. People over sixty were at greater risk. His sons reminded him he was no longer in his fifties. He should leave.

This embarrassed him, the implication of weakness. It angered him too, but in the silly way he had been angry whenever coaches took him out of a football game—even when they were way ahead. He had no symptoms, but there was that COPD. Some of his friends were sick, not dying, but he had a bad feeling about that. His wife was on her screens and phones all day with clients clamoring for stimulus packages. She could do that anywhere with good Wi-Fi.

So they were leaving, and now he had the rented Suburban. *Dawn patrol*, he thought, but just him. No Irma teaching him how to see, no sons coming slowly awake. The sun was rising where the Twin Towers had been, behind One WTC, now Freedom Tower, as no one he knew ever called it. He had seen it fall. He turned left on Warren, crossed over to City Hall Park and then back uptown on Lafayette, driving slowly. The traffic was very light, the streets almost clear. An aphorism from Black September edged into his thinking: *The slower you move, the faster you die.*

Big Cove Tannery

His hair was over his ears. That was fast. He shopped online for a wood-burning tool and started notching the days on a gnarled sycamore branch he found in the woods.

His road dead-ended at Lick Run, a creek now almost a river with the early spring runoff. All around were rolling hills sectioned with working farms, carpeted with hay grasses. An occasional silo poked the horizon. He knew that living here did not make him a farmer. His privilege draped over him like his worn Filson jacket. He was like the people he read about fleeing to country houses or the Hamptons, except he was in a farmhouse 250 miles west of Manhattan in Big Cove Tannery, PA. The Mason-Dixon Line. Battlefield ghosts everywhere. There were Confederate flags in the yards of the poorest trailers. If he needed any guns, he could pick them up at a shop six miles away in West Virginia. Everyone was friendly behind their loose social distancing. He saw only white people. Mostly poor white people. Farmers. He pictured Irma catching her brother's fastballs and curves in front of the barn on the farm in Solon Springs.

His wife told him about hedge funds looking to draw down billion-dollar credit lines. He looked up the per capita income in his new county: $26,082. Cases of Covid-19: 19; Deaths: 1. On Zoom he deflected conversations away from any details of his life. He would glide over questions about what he was up to—like writing this sentence. Driving here he had been aware of his freedom, feeling the exaltation of being on the move. This was the opposite.

Every morning he sat in a creaky wooden rocking chair on his rented two-hundred-year-old colonial porch. He was the center of his own little world. When he made himself the center of things as a little boy, Irma would ask him how he thought other people felt, like the kid who was not even good enough to play right field, or the girl who never talked. He tried but did not have the language to describe what he was thinking, even to himself. Now he had so much language it felt ponderous. What could he say? He was not the center of the universe, after all.

Determined to count his blessings, he followed his dog, the two of them mammals together in the gentle woods. Neither worried or even particularly alert. No lurking dangers, no excitement except in his head, replaying a day he had walked a sand riverbed at Mana Pools looking for wild dogs. Maybe it was the flattening heat or the quiet of nothing else moving or the tow of childhood ghosts . . . Then, finally and astonishingly, the dogs, painted dogs, with orange patches overlapping black spots, yellow ear tufts and underparts with a whitish throat mane—unchanged since the Middle Pleistocene. This may sound very strange to you. It was to him, kinetically, profoundly strange, right there in Big Cove Tannery.

Masks

He started painting, something he had not done since college. He remembered the fresh excitement of his art classes, and Irma telling him he should paint for fun, and how unexpected that had been. He remembered studying Salvador Dalí, whose art he did not like, but still: "Every morning upon awakening, I experience a supreme pleasure: that of being Salvador Dalí, and I ask myself, wonder-struck, what prodigious thing will he do today, this Salvador Dalí."

That did it.

He drove forty miles to the kind of huge arts-and-crafts outlet that did not exist when he first bought art supplies, and quickly spent $300. He did not think about it. Back on his porch, he worked all afternoon stretching ten canvases and laying out his paints and brushes. It was fun.

He did not miss the city, but he missed his friends and thought if he made paintings for them it would hold them together in some way. The paintings would be of Lakota masks, like he had seen at the Museum of the Plains Indian in Browning. He would be careful to get the masks right, especially the eyes and horns. He tried to match the illustrative style of the Indian book Irma had given him when he was a Cub Scout, and it surprised him that he was still able to control his acrylics.

His next step was to paint Covid masks on the Lakota masks. He worked fast, and the paintings came together quickly. He punched up the obvious symbolism with the heavy paint he laid on with a palette knife and in some places with a goose feather he had found that left a delicate texture on the canvases. The backgrounds were all variations of his journal brain drawings, full of snakes and bats and tiny dragons but also birds and fish and insects. He wanted his masks to hum.

When he packed and mailed out the paintings, his enclosed note was the same to all the friends: "Here is one in a series of *NINE MASKS in the Second Spring of COVID* and images of the other eight." He added a separate note explaining the paintings were going up on Rarible as a set of crypto assets. That said, his friends would own their original until they gave it away or whatever. That was his story of his masks.

The Lakota story of their mask starts when the Lakota roamed the Plains hunting buffalo and lived a happy life. He learned this by reading a Lakota scribe named Tracey (no last name) who explained sadly that there were also times when they had to go against another people and do things they normally would not do. Warriors would go to a sweat lodge where an elder would reach into his medicine bag and pull out imaginary masks for each of them. When the elder gave a warrior a mask, he also gave what would be needed in battle—fearlessness, agility, strength. When the warriors returned, the Elder would take each man's imaginary mask and put it back in his medicine bag to rid him of all he had seen, all the bad things, all their thoughts and actions would go back in the bag and his experiences in battle were no longer a part of him. He was again a compassionate, kindhearted man who could hold his children without the ghosts of bad things lurking behind him. Tracey did not explain when the Lakota started making physical representations of the masks.

He would make more mask paintings for his friends. It would be fun.

Sycamore

There was old weather on his face. He had lived three of Bob's life-times. Old men were supposed to be wise. Not in his experience. It was not as if men had had nothing to teach him. He could still summon the relief of Chesterfield tobacco on his bee sting, and he had used it once on Thomas. But he learned more from women if he paid attention, and he was observant. Irma had taught him that, along with the trees and birds.

Norm had just fucked with him, not listening, bullying, lying about his real estate deals, answering only his own questions, shit-ting on everyone who did not look like him. Norm's malevolence still dogged him, pulling him back—what kind of a man grabs his ten-year-old stepson by the balls as a joke? Irma was a survivor, and maybe a survivor is what he was too, but there were so many meaner stories than his, unbearable sometimes. And Irma had pre-vailed, not just survived. She had built something for herself. Her life had flowered with a house she loved and travel and a final, solid marriage to a man she liked.

Remembering her now was getting to know her in a new way, recognizing what she had given him. He decided some ideas take years to pop, lifetimes even. You make a mental note about something and it comes back decades later fully formed—and you recognize what was disguised when you first looked. Irma had set him up for that one morning when she was reading to him on the cinder-block step in Burbank and had stopped to explain the verb *to disguise*. "A good word for you," she said, with a wink. Irma was cocky.

Nothing would have scared him more than seeing her unsure and girlish, frightened, and she never showed him any of that. That was something she must have thought about, like sending him off by simply letting him go. Some mothers believe there is a certain life for an only son, a particular career perhaps, and even a woman somewhere meant for his wife, and they already know all about her, her looks, her family, the kind of a mother she will be. Irma was nothing like that, and she had left him with no fear except of the loss of place, whatever was gone, what was not there anymore. California all those years ago. So many birds. The trees.

He got up earlier and earlier, taking longer and longer walks. He learned the local trees—the red oaks, the pines, the birches—and saw many that he had known as a boy in California. His new favorites were sycamore that grew to 130 feet with gray-brown outer bark that peeled off in patches to reveal the light gray or white wood beneath. They had fan-shaped leaves and bright red seed pods and were meant to symbolize longevity, clarity, eternity, but they were just trees too. The one beyond the porch was two hundred years old and attracted goldfinch and black-capped chickadee. As spring opened into summer, more and more birds arrived. Not just the idea of birds.

The skylarks, song thrushes, and robins woke him before light.

He heard turkeys and woodpeckers all day. From his porch he watched swallows and bluebirds building nests across the road. At night in bed he listened to nightingales and barred owls and nighthawks, and one dawn, a night heron he could not further identify. The beauty of the world was dazzlingly, vividly unbearable. The beautiful strangeness of being alive.

The field behind the farmhouse was still unmowed, high with hay grass. He walked the field many times, sometimes in the rain. There were some loose boards and cut branches along a fence. One day he got down on his hands and knees. The earth was soft and damp. He started to dig.

He would always have a fort.

Witness

The next afternoon, after walking all morning and a peach for lunch, he sat in his fort and let it all go. It was Irma's "Que Sera, Sera," but more than that. Excavations of his past were no longer necessary, his memories like dreams of random recall, people and places with no order, like broken glass, now coming into focus with less dissembling, less self-justification. Not random at all.

He felt gently rebuked. How strange he had been in his child-hood, crawling through fields on his tough little paws. Now here he was sitting in a little boy's fort, grown older and stranger still, more altered by the small experiences he remembered of his childhood than the milestones of his adult life. His privilege had been unspo-ken, expected to carry him until he faded with age into some cow-boy movie sunset or, better, went down clean without lingering in anyone's care. It was enough just to be a man—as long as you were a white man. The racism and misogyny ran deep, but he was hopeful. There would be a new reality. There would have to be. Races, ages, and genders standing together, fists raised with hope beneath the rage, not the mania and despair of the 1960s, the exhaustion of bro-ken ideas. The narratives were being scrapped over, but inequities would be addressed. Something beautiful made out of ugly things.

He watched a spider crawl over his boot. *Iktomi*, trickster-healer, thunder dreamer, contrary warrior-clown, *crazy in a sacred way* . . . He had had no idea that time would accelerate, or that he would not be the same person every day. What did that mean? He had no idea, but it did not bother him anymore. He knew enough—the taste of his peach, the way the river jetty reached into the Pacific. Maybe he would find a new place, on a coast somewhere, where fields dropped to rough water. A place where he could walk an edge. Nova Scotia or Wales or somewhere he had never seen. Or what about right here where he was sitting on this rich, sandy soil? This fine, beautiful dirt. Anywhere, really.

So yes, he was hopeful, a happy monkey climbing a tree. There would be no die-off. The pandemic would end. The world would open. Ending the climate crisis would mean everything because that is what was at stake. Everything. And everything was connected to everything else and everything could be explained by everything else. There was redemption in that, something to pass on to his sons—not the secrets of some men's hut but the responsibility of witness, the privilege of it. He would die for his sons. That is what he wanted his life to mean. He knew what he was doing. He was a witness. He remembered the births of his sons. *A privileged witness.*

You just had to look and see, you had to put the robin's nest back in the lilac bush. Irma had taught him that. It took courage, of course, and he remembered the PTA meeting all those years before, when Irma was introduced as a new teacher and he had hoped that even if he and Irma and Norm were not a regular family maybe they were not that different from everyone else. On the way home, Irma had asked if something was bothering him. He could not answer, but there was something, and not knowing gave him a terrible feeling. Irma slowed the Ford and said she knew something good that Bob had told her. He thought maybe he was going to cry.

"It's better not to be like everyone else," Irma said.

She had made that up for him and it became his life, being different, trying to express himself as an artist and writer and even, he hoped now, as a human being. He was Irma's son and the most important things he knew he had learned from her. He would remember that and it would make him a better man. He would do the right thing. He knew it like he had known it as a little boy, since right now, then . . . He watched the light change.

His breathing lengthened.

Part III

...

FLOYD BENNETT FIELD

1

(PLEASURE POINT)

If you let yourself go, you can follow your thoughts to a new place. I see now, he told himself, that I am not finished . . .

Irma

When I think of Irma now, I think of her blondeness, and her quick blue eyes, and her white skin, translucent not pale. She had what was called a good figure. She was not vain about it, but she did not hide it either. She was slender with surprising breasts and beautiful legs like the movie stars of the 1940s she was compared to—Betty Grable and Lana Turner. She always felt soft when I was a little boy. Later, I saw the strength of an athlete. She was good at golf and tennis, which she played with Bob. She liked football because it was my sport, and hockey because Bob had played in college, but baseball was her sport.

She was good at cards, any game. She was not good at telling jokes, but she laughed easily and quietly. She read aloud with subtle inflection and beautiful emotion, unusual even for a primary school teacher. She read to children every day of the fifty years she taught. She had a pitch pipe and played simple songs on the piano. Her penmanship was perfect.

Her clothes were stylish in a department-store kind of way. She seldom wore pants. She could sew, and made shirts for me when I was in grammar school and she was still substituting. She was a good cook and took advantage of the fruits and vegetables she had not tasted before arriving in the Santa Clara Valley. She loved artichokes, as soon as she figured them out, and experimented with sauces. She became especially good at enchiladas and tacos. She baked peach pies from scratch on my birthdays.

She liked cars and drove fast and was not at all timid when the freeways came. When it was hot, she drove with her elbow out the window. Her perfume was Tailspin by Lucien Lelong. Top notes: citruses, cloves, gardenia, hyacinth; base notes: ambergris, patchouli, pine. I looked it up. She drank highballs and beer, but only wine after Norm was gone. She never smoked.

She was unhurried, although she was busy and energetic. Those around her found this calming, as I had as a child with so much energy she would sometimes ask me if my hair was on fire. Her favorite color was blue, like mine. And Bob's, she told me. Irma loved Bob more than she ever loved anyone, even me. I know because she told me that too, to make me happy.

I never saw her cry.

"Hey, Good Lookin'"

Bob had a dog named Colonel and a 1938 Ford when he courted Irma. There are many photographs of them with that car and playing with that dog. The Ford was a black V-8, with running boards, and Colonel was a sheepdog. I also know they met in college at the University of Minnesota, Duluth, in 1940 and took drives in the country and along the shore of Lake Superior. Their song was "Hey Good Lookin'" from Cole Porter's 1942 musical *Something for the Boys*. Jack told me Bob liked to sing the lyrics when he and Irma were driving around:

> *Hey, hey, hey, hey, good-lookin'*
> *Give in and we'll begin cookin'*
> *That delish*
> *Little dish*
> *Called love*

I do not know what Irma thought when Hank Williams's rewritten version was released in 1951. Hank lived in Bakersfield and "Hey, Good Lookin'" by Hank and his band, the Drifting Cowboys, was all over California radio. We heard it when we were driving around looking at real estate with Norm. When Bo Diddley released his version in 1965, Irma was seeing the guy in the National Guard. When the movie *Hey, Good Lookin'* came out in 1982 she had just met Carl.

I do not know where Irma and Bob were married, but I know it was not in a church. I do not know how I would know this except from Fronie, who might have said something about not being invited to the wedding. I have seen no wedding pictures.

If you look up why couples elope, you will read that they want a totally intimate wedding celebration—a day focused on just the two of them without the pressure, anxiety, and obligation of a traditional wedding. In 1941, I am not so sure. There could have been many reasons. When I was a very little boy, Irma would tease, telling me every mother has secrets from her son and she did too, although that was usually about Christmas presents.

A popular joke line was about nagging mothers harassing sons for not calling them to stay in touch. The son would finally call and the mother would never hang up. I never got the joke, or any of the attendant Jewish mother jokes about food or whatever. Most sons pull away as they grow into manhood, sharing less, but Irma and I carried on. As I grew older, I called Irma more and more. Our conversations became increasingly about Nick and Thomas, with detours into how it could be that this or that politician was so stupid or that some dumbass developer had finally cut down the giant walnut tree on the way to Los Gatos and put in yet another car wash.

The jokes I remember Irma liking were not so much jokes as running gags she watched on *I Love Lucy* once we got a television set. She never laughed out loud but would smile and nod slightly as Lucy messed with people's heads by wanting more than marriage and motherhood. Lucy's hijinks getting in and out of trouble—but never having to be saved—were underlined by Lucille Ball's physical comedy, which I thought Irma could have mimicked if she felt like it. She was that graceful.

The show Irma could not stand was *My Friend Irma*, which came up often for obvious reasons. "Irma" was a featherbrained stenographer from Minnesota who mangled whatever her boss dictated, and got ditzier as the episodes rolled out. Her simple-minded adventures almost always ended in tears.

Irma's own humor, how she made me laugh, was deadpan, like on Nick's third birthday, when I asked her what I had been like at that age.

"I didn't know who you were yet," Irma said.

I do not think Irma ever lied to me. That was one of our deals, and I remember the exact moment. It was early morning and we were leaving Duluth for California and had just gotten into the Ford with Nana and Pops watching from the porch. Before she turned the key in the ignition, Irma smiled over at me and said that the most important thing from then on was that we always tell each other the truth. No matter what, we could never lie. At the time, I did not think I had ever lied and probably barely understood what lying was, but I understood it was a new rule. I could not have known that Irma would enforce it over and over in such subtle ways that it would live in my little-boy head like a gentle echo until I was out of her house.

When I was older I wondered if Irma was being pragmatic

because lying just postponed the inevitable, just put things off. "Just a waste of time," is what she would say. In more lucid moments I thought that not lying, especially to herself, had a lot to do with why Irma did not believe in luck—luck was a big lie. What I believe now is that Irma simply believed good guys did not lie and wanted me to be one too.

Irma wanted me to be more than an observant child. Before I was in kindergarten, she told me that was the way to feel grown-up. She said she was telling me what she told all her first graders: that they could pay attention and still not hear because they were listening too hard. It was the same with seeing. They could look as hard as they could and still not see unless they were open to surprises, alert to whatever might come next. Something for me to think about. Did I like surprises?

"Like that guy with the long tail," Irma said, pointing out the window at a squirrel running along a walnut tree branch overhanging the intersection where we were stopped at a red light. There was always something, and I was always in training.

She wanted me to remember things, to grow up to be the kind of serious man who knew something about the world and could stand up and tell people what he thought without showing off. The kind of a man who stood up for people, especially women when it came to that. The kind of man who liked women.

I knew from the beginning that men liked Irma, although I had only vague ideas what that meant at the time or, later, what it ever meant to her. Her attitude seemed to be that men and women were just different and that was not good or bad. They did not have to understand each other to get along—and that was sexy.

We seldom talked about her boyfriends except sometimes after they were gone, when a name would come up and she would roll her eyes and say that she did not know what she had been thinking. What I saw, though, was that she liked them all, although she certainly did not need them. I note too that they were all in great physical shape for their ages, and she outlived them all.

At some point Irma decided she would not let the past be all she had. She was not just a pretty Midwestern girl, the kind who got lost looking for a better life in California—and she did not. She went from substitute teaching to what California used to call a Master Teacher, designing curricula and helping to discredit IQ tests. She went from broke widow to making enough money in real estate to retire on a cliff overlooking the Pacific. This took a lot, courage most of all.

Her happiness was never something I thought about. I figured she had to be happy with the way things were working out. I think she also knew it was not enough for her just to keep working on a better life—whatever that may have meant to her. I know she remembered earlier versions of herself very clearly and that her childhood was much harder than she let me know. That was one way she took good care of me, and I took good care of my turtle and my goldfish because if I did not feed them they would starve to death. Irma and I talked a lot about that when I was little, about responsibility.

She never said so, but I think Irma thought she was a good mother and liked that about herself. As a child, I did not know there is nothing as terrifying as a bad mother, but when I had sons of my own, it spooked me to see young mothers shouting and swatting their children in grocery stores and on playgrounds and yanking them in and out of cabs. I also learned that some mothers haunt their children with complaints in wide categories from things being too expensive to girlfriends/boyfriends to *will you miss me when I'm gone?* With some mothers it is so bad their children say they will not have children until their mother is dead. When I hear things like that, I think about Irma sending books and teaching my sons to spin flour tortillas.

Tahoe

Irma had an overcast side that I seldom saw as a child, and never saw after I reached my teens, but it was there. I know because she showed me, although I did not understand until I was as old as Irma was at the time. Something had happened with Norm about money, and she was tense in the quiet way that bothered me because I knew a bad argument was coming.

Norm had just gotten his Cadillac. Irma and I were on summer vacation. It was coming up on the Fourth of July, and two of my friends were going camping at Lake Tahoe with their families. I asked Irma if we could go camping sometime too, and just like that we were going to Lake Tahoe. Irma called the fathers for particulars of which campground and what to bring, but it seemed to me that we just got in the car with my sleeping bag and left. Irma did not say goodbye to Norm, and we drove over Donner Pass with the top down.

The campground was crowded with cars and tents and I slept on the ground next to the Ford and Irma slept in the back seat. We had a grill at our little campsite so we could cook the hot dogs Irma brought, but the toilet was a long walk, and close to the campsites my friends' dads had reserved way in advance. When we went there the second night for a campfire, the dads were glad to see us, but the mothers did not seem very happy. There was no good place for Irma to sit, so she drank a beer standing up and went back to the Ford. She said I could stay for a while if I wanted, but pretty soon I went back to the Ford too.

Irma sat in the front passenger seat with the door open and I sat on the ground in front of her while she drank one of the Millers she had brought. We were leaving first thing in the morning. I said maybe we could go to the Custer Battlefield at Little Bighorn, but that was too far. Sometimes things just go wrong. Irma must have seen that I did not understand, and how disappointed I was.

"We're a lot alike" is all Irma said.

Norm

Cleaning out a storage room in a warehouse in Long Island City, I found ten boxes from Irma, sent twenty-five years before, never opened. I looked at smudged report cards and tarnished sports trophies with no memory of achievement—surprised that Irma had saved them. I peered at class photographs and yearbooks and wondered who those people were. How unremarkable we all looked.

There was also a baby book, a photo album, and a small Bible inscribed *to Irma from The Sunday School, Dec. 25, 1929.* She was ten. The photographs were mostly of Irma and me—on a Florida beach smiling with a little sand shovel and bucket; smiling with a black farmhand and a mule in an orange grove; smiling with a strange-looking Santa Claus in a department store. Always smiling. I had no memory of any of it. The pictures of Irma showed off her figure in smart, square-shouldered jackets. Others showed her in college, fresh and athletic, and there was a high school portrait with her hair bobbed.

The baby book was "Baby's First Seven Years," published by the University of Chicago, and described on the title page as of practical service to the mother and the growing child. Then, on page four:

POSITION AT DELIVERY (BREECH, ETC.): Turned wrong way.

DURATION OF LABOR: 12 hours.

TYPE OF PAIN RELIEF FOR MOTHER: None.

I had never been told anything about my birth except that Pops gave the stork a big tip.

Norm was there too—his bullshit division patch from the Persian Gulf Command, and a photograph of Irma kissing him. I wondered why Irma had sent it. Norm looked handsome. I opened my phone, found him dead in Santa Clara, April 22, 2001.

At home that night I went deep into the census: Norman Adolph Elden, born August 4, 1919, in St. Croix, Wisconsin. Adolph was there, dead at eighty in Duluth, 1964. The surprise was Constance Teresa Dahl Elden (1885–1927), Norm's mother, dead at forty-two when Norm was eight. His grandmother died three years later, when Norm was eleven. Adolph was a railroad laborer, born in Norway, arrived in America in 1917. Ten years later, he was raising a son, poor and alone. That was how Norm grew up.

The past was always hiding things, like Norm raised motherless by Adolph. Maybe Irma loved him for that. And Bob knew it, and now I knew it too, even as I knew everything Norm said and did as a husband and father was a threat. If Norm were forty now, nothing about him would be acceptable.

Even his attempts at fatherhood were pathetic—giving me a shitty softball mitt he said had been used by the famous Yankee shortstop Phil Rizzuto. When I wanted a puppy, Norm took an aging collie off the hands of a realtor in his office he was looking to split a commission with and said it was Lassie's brother when he brought it home. It was almost funny.

I never thought Irma was afraid of Norm, but she forgave him with too many second chances. He terrorized us both like a 1950s cartoon of what men were supposed to be. Norm never thought about any of that and I still hate him for it. My anger is bone-hard, comforting like a familiar scar. It is always there, like a line that stays with me from Christopher Logue's *War Music* translation of Homer's *Iliad*: *Horsemen ride out of the tree line and down into a stream somewhere in Kansas or Missouri, say.*

Irma

Irma was old suddenly, the way it happens to beautiful women. She stopped having her hair done every Friday morning, and moved her bed to the big room on the first floor, facing the glass wall looking out over Pleasure Point. She said she enjoyed watching the surfers and was noticing things about the kelp beds she had not seen before. She knew she was fading, and apologized for her hair when I arrived. I was there a week, the days creeping past while Irma mostly slept. On Sunday, we watched the NFL.

I worked on my laptop in a chair next to her bed. Irma asked if I remembered being a little boy. I did, very much, but I just smiled and nodded.

"What?" She was not smiling.

I started with riding my Phantom and the orchards and my sports and school. I said I liked school, and the peach pies on my birthdays. Going to Kirk's without Norm, but I did not say his name.

"But what?" Irma said. "What did you like best?"

"You," I said, thinking I would surprise her.

"No," she said, not surprised. "You had no choice about me."

I told her I remembered the way things looked, the birds and the different trees and all the other things she showed me how to see in the Santa Clara Valley in 1950. I told her that was why I could see beauty everywhere, not just the view of Pleasure Point out her bay window—the Pacific stretching west all the way to the perfect plum gardens in Japan's Ibaraki Prefecture. It was a game I played with her, tossing in obscure geographic details no matter how distant from my experience, just something I had heard or read about.

She asked me if I had read about the couple who took their baby son with them on home invasions in suburban Connecticut. I had not.

"At least we didn't do that," she said.

We laughed. That was her half of the game, strange bits of news, her *tidbits*, as she called them.

"You should go," Irma said. "Get out of here. Come back next month. I'll let you know."

"What does that mean?"

"I can't believe I'm eighty-five years old."

"Your mother lived to a hundred and three."

"Your sister is coming . . ."

Irma closed her eyes. I wanted to tell her that sometimes I would sneak out my bedroom window at night and walk in the dark orchards. The trees were that close, and there I was again, sitting in my fort with a sudden, enduring knowledge. *Nothingness.*

Irma died in that room a week after I returned to New York. My half sister, Cheryl, was there, with Irma's nurse and housekeeper.

IRMA

Cheryl was calm on the phone. She told me Irma closed her eyes for the last time looking out her window at the Pacific. She had Irma cremated and sent half of the ashes to me. Her half she took out on a friend's fishing boat and scattered over the kelp beds off Pleasure Point. There was no other service. All Irma's friends were dead.

Jack

When Jack knew he was on his way out, he sent me a package of clippings about Bob's death. Jack had never said Bob was a fighter pilot, and I was always afraid to ask, somehow knowing that Bob's real story would not be my story of Bob. I guess Jack thought I knew, thought Irma had told me.

Bob died in a plane crash near the Naval Air Station at Norfolk on January 5, 1945. He had never been in the Pacific or flown F4F Wildcats off carriers. He flew tow targets behind modified C-47s for the Atlantic Fleet. Never a fighter pilot. I'd made all that up and Irma had gone along.

The navy blamed the crash on "motor trouble." There was a death certificate: "Injuries multiple extreme due to plane crash." The newspaper accounts reported that "Lieutenant Commander McDonell, who was the pilot, maneuvered the plane to avoid crashing into two buildings, both of which were occupied . . ." Jack's letter said Bob was a bigger hero. The newspapers did not say that one of those buildings was a hospital. Bob's copilot and crew of four enlisted men all died with him. I looked up the day. It was a Friday. Bob had just turned twenty-five. I was five months old.

———

Jack's plane was a B-24 heavy bomber called *Buzz Job*, with a cartoonish wasp with an oversized stinger painted just behind the nose gunner's turret, under Jack's pilot-side window. When Jack was dying in a fancy assisted living facility, his sons hung a perfect model of *Buzz Job* from the ceiling above his bed.

I had written to Jack when he moved into that place. Its website noted pride in care and the hospitality of the staff, organizing events so there was always something for everyone to enjoy. I complimented Jack on his smart move—very pleasant and practical—and suggested he was probably meeting some interesting "new friends." I used the quote marks to let him know it was me. He wrote back: "Ha!"

Pops had died in the same kind of place, just not as nice.

I spent an afternoon there with Jack the week he died. He was in and out, sometimes lucid, other times just staring up at his plane. When I was leaving, Jack called me Bob, then caught himself and said I was the man of the family now, then stalled again and said I should take care of Irma if something happened to Bob. It had been seventy-two years since Bob went down; Irma dead for twelve.

Irma

They say literature gives you license, and memoir lets you lie. Why bother if you are not in it to preserve reputation, which I am not. That kid in Cheyenne is still with me, and so is the cowboy at the rodeo and Irma leaving me in the motel with the bronc rider waving his hat. I remember more and more—a radio announcer saying it is one hundred degrees and Irma is driving us across Nevada wearing blue capris and the white Spaldings she liked, with bobby socks and a little scarf tied around her neck . . . and how she is too young.

My share of Irma's ashes stayed with me, packed with my books for every move. I meant to scatter them but could not decide where, or maybe I could not let go. No one knew about any of this, or that I was writing about it.

Finishing this chapter, I put the manuscript away. I was not ready. I am not trying to be tricky. It was too personal, too much information. Bob would have been one hundred years old that month.

Ten days later, I chartered a twenty-eight-foot Whaler and scattered Irma's ashes on Jamaica Bay, just off Floyd Bennett Field. It was windy, and Irma was blown across the whitecaps.

"I love you," I told her, for the first time.

✦ ✦ ✦

Coda

I am not sure what Irma would think of this book. She would not have objected, but that does not mean she would not have had her own take on what I was up to. Maybe she would remember telling me to write "like the writers you like," and have an opinion about that. She would keep it to herself, of course.

Wanting to please her after she was gone started a run of second guesses. Maybe I was intimidated by social media. The idea, just the idea, of writing about my life in the middle of that swamp made me tentative, unreliable, *full of bologna*. *Off.* Or maybe I sensed it was not my turn to talk, or even wave. And then, preposterously, maybe I was too white and too old and too straight to have anything to say about women, even my mother. I have yet to get over that.

When I had started writing, the working title was *Trouble in Mind*, and it was going to be about me—about how it was for me as a little boy, and how I took my chances over the years, constantly revising the circuitry (extra research) of my memory. That changed with the help of friends and editors who unanimously agreed that Irma was more interesting.

It is hard to get outside of what you already know about yourself, and that is not the way I had ever thought about writing, but the classic writer's desire to talk endlessly about himself or herself started slipping away and was then suddenly gone. I was no longer a student of my own history, rather a son finding his way to fifty thousand words about the most important person in his life.

Irma told me once that friends were important to her because she had so few of them growing up on the farm in Solon Springs. That was hard for me to imagine because in California after Norm was gone she had plenty of friends, mostly women, mostly other teachers. I have a memory of several of them sitting in Irma's backyard in Campbell drinking dry Chablis and laughing that women made the best friends. I wish I had known enough to write about them, but then it would not have mattered one way or another to Irma. My oversight was more obvious anyway: my sister.

I did not write that my sister's middle name is Noreen, after Norm, her father. I was gone by the time she was nine, and we have been barely in touch since, although we are somehow close enough to joke that we communicate primarily by rumor. That was Irma's joke about us. It is from the play and film *A Thousand Clowns* starring Jason Robards, whom Irma liked because of his World War II navy service. Anyway, Cheryl and I got the joke, and that was fine. Irma was disappointed but not surprised. And I think that still hangs over the two of us.

Like me, Cheryl left Campbell after high school, released by Irma to find her own way, also like me. After graduating from

Sonoma State, she married a good man, a musician, moved to the Russian River, and had a daughter she named Sophronia, after Irma and Fronie. She worked through a successful career as a health-care executive until retiring early to a small ranch deeper into Northern California. I do not know if she could send our mother messages just by thinking them but probably.

Cheryl remembers eating scrambled eggs with ketchup out of small yellow bowls when we lived on Patch Ave. Norm didn't like the way I ate and made me finish my dinner in the garage with the dog. And another time Norm pushing Irma down the street with her arm behind her back and then standing over her shouting that he couldn't take it anymore. Norm ripped the phone out of the wall and threw it through the window. She was nine wearing a party dress that Irma made for her. It was blue velvet.

Cheryl had her own story with Irma, who I know showed her how to dig for worms and bait a hook to fish for bluegill, and she knew her trees and birds. Prom dresses and first boyfriends had to be part of their mix of bonds and secrets. I know by blood that Irma raised her to look hard at things too, and to take care of her family, do whatever had to be done—courage as inheritance, a passed-down thing.

When I was not around, Cheryl was right there for Irma. She visited Pleasure Point regularly and was at Irma's bedside at the end—certainly as close/closer to Irma as/than I had ever been. Irma would have wanted that in this picture. So do I.

Not long before I finished *Irma*, I read that the New York Botanical Garden's majestic Himalayan pine was dead, struck by lightning.

I knew that tree, with its graceful, pendulous branches and long, silvery-green cones. Arborists determined that the great tree, which had grown to eighty feet since it was planted in 1903, was beyond saving. I was sad and remember thinking it would have made Irma sad too. There was comfort in that, and a fierce joy.

Author's Note

This book is a book about my mother and me, but it is also about memory and getting things right and wrong. I want to come straight at this: sourcing and attribution can be tricky in memoirs, depending on what the author actually remembers. In my case, memories changed (evolved?) way beyond the classic definition of an unreliable narrator. That said, there is no malice. Some names have been disguised for personal reasons. Any mistakes are mine alone.

From my early twenties I kept diaries and day books, filling them with notes and scraps of writing both mine and what I admired in my reading. The Web changed that, but even as I worked online, I kept my own paper trail, scrapbooks really, with photos and business cards and matchbooks and bits of nature (flowers, shells) pasted in among my notes. Writing *Irma*, I looked at all of this and was surprised at the incoherence.

More often I was online, checking my memory against infinite trails of information about, say, the Santa Clara Valley. I also cruised my favorite writers looking for remembered passages and finding new ideas. I made new notes but also copied and pasted, including from my own old notes, the ones I had made thinking that they might be useful later—for what I wasn't sure. (Almost all journalists work this way.) The result is now something I am publishing as mine, an *aggregation* with many debts to what was reported, written, and thought before me; and I want to give proper credit. If I overlooked an appropriate attribution or somehow conflated something, I welcome the opportunity to correct any unintended sloppiness.

My use of "*Arf!*" on page 153, however, is a direct steal from Thomas McGuane's second novel *The Bushwhacked Piano* (Simon & Schuster, 1971). I have never taken anything else, but his writing has informed my literary taste and judgment for fifty years. His longtime friend Jim Harrison, whom I met (on the phone) the same day I met McGuane, is the other bookend on that longest shelf in my library. Harrison is known for many works of fiction and non-fiction but was fundamentally a poet and finishing these pages I returned almost daily to his poetry (Jim Harrison, *Complete Poems*, Copper Canyon Press, 2021).

For generations now, writing in America as a man meant dealing one way or another with Ernest Hemingway's literary manliness with all its fallibility. I not only read the work but was encouraged to study it. The definitions of fatherhood are a central braid in this book, and I believe Ernest got it all wrong; and the virulence of the manhood he defined remains harmful. I spent some years thinking about this, beginning in 1996 when I was hired to write a miniseries off of his posthumous memoir *A Moveable Feast*. After I'd done significant research and written several drafts I was fired, and another writer took a crack at it. (The miniseries was never made.) Except for the money, I did not care. Hemingway disappointed over and over. That is the thing about Ernest, there are too many things you do not want to know. Much more recently my thinking is significantly informed by two brilliant biographies: Paul Hendrickson's *Hemingway's Boat: Everything He Loved in Life, and Lost, 1934–1961* (Alfred A. Knopf, 2011); and Mary Dearborn's *Hemingway, A Biography* (Knopf, 2017). That said, I in no way mean to imply that my harsh judgment of Ernest reflects theirs.

I read a great deal about writing and *The Paris Review*'s ongoing "Writers at Work" series was invaluable. When it came to the spookiness and responsibility of it (writing), Katie Roiphe's "Art of Nonfiction No.4, Interview with Janet Malcolm" (Spring, 2011) was profound, especially what does and does not "quite make it onto the page." Susan Minot's *Why I Don't Write and Other Stories* (Vintage, 2021) made me think more rigorously about writing and memory. When it came to best practices, Verlyn Klinkenborg's *Several Short Sentences About Writing* (Knopf, 2012) is straight-up brilliant.

I also read widely about fathers and stepfathers, and found Ann Patchett's "My Three Fathers" (*The New Yorker*, Sept. 28, 2020) at once clean-spirited and sharply honest in a way I wanted to emulate. *This Boy's Life* by Tobias Wolff is the classic. At the same time I returned to Homer's *Iliad*, specifically the translations of Christopher Logue in this order: *War Music: An Account of Books 16 to 19 of Homer's* Iliad (Farrar, Straus and Giroux, 1987); *All Day Permanent Red: The First Battle Scenes of Homer's* Iliad, (Farrar, Straus and Giroux, 2004); *The Husbands: An Account of Books 3 and 4 of Homer's* Iliad (Farrar, Straus and Giroux, 1995); *Cold Calls: War Music Continued* (Gardners Books, 2005). I refuse to speculate about why I was so drawn to them but I was. And also to Pat Barker's *The Silence of the Girls* (Doubleday Books, 2018).

The Eve Ensler interview I refer on page 178 was a "By the Book" column of the *New York Times Book Review* (May 26, 2019).

Author's Note

The *Esquire* Editor's Letter I refer to on page 114 is "Girls in the Office," (March 1993).

My novel *California Bloodstock* (MacMillan Publishers, 1981) carries an epilogue from Joan Didion: "California is someplace else." It is from "Notes from a Native Daughter" in Didion's early book, *Slouching Towards Bethlehem* (Farrar, Straus and Giroux, 1968) and has been in my head continuously since it came out. Like generations of writers from California, I am still informed by her original thinking about our state as well as her perfect words. When she died everyone moved up one. (Jack Nicholson said the same thing about Marlon Brando.) Rachel Kushner's "The Hard Crowd: Coming of Age on the Streets of San Francisco," which she first published as a Personal History in the *New Yorker* (January 18, 2021), helped me clarify my own experience even though I grew up two generations ahead of her in a very different California.

California is at the heart of this book. I do not mean only the devastation that comes with subdividing the land that I knew as a little boy. As Joy Williams says, "Landscapes are emotional." Over my time at UC Irvine, I met artists who changed the way I saw landscapes and gave me the *idea* of art as *ideas*. Frank Stella was there with his then wife, the young critic Barbara Rose. David Hockney came through and taught drawing for what seemed like only a few seconds, but there were emerging artists everywhere. The gang of young minimalists I refer to on page 74 included John McCracken, Robert Irwin, Larry Bell, Phil Kaufman, and was led by the slightly older Tony Delap who named his beautifully crafted pieces after wizards and magicians. In my first studio class with him, Delap told me to "mess around for a while and maybe you'll do one." That is still my ambition.

Acknowledgments

My wife, Stacey Hadash, is my first reader. Then Nick McDonell and Thomas McDonell (who also conceived the cover).

I also turn to my friends. Antonio Weiss was precise and intuitive as he is in all things. Lorraine Adams and Richard Price gave me encouragement at just the right time. Susan Casey, a superb editor and writer as well as an old friend reminded me you can always go deeper. Longtime colleague Bob Roe did hard, early work with the incisive chops he is known for. Robin Desser gave me thoughtful, extensive notes. As always, Morgan Entrekin was excellent counsel.

My friend and agent, Amanda Urban, the unsung editor of so many books it is an in-joke among her clients, showed me what I should be writing about when I thought this book was about me.

Finally, and importantly, I am more than grateful to Sara Nelson, my editor at HarperCollins, who recognized traps and opportunities in the manuscript, and then pulled it all together with intelligence and grace. I am not sure where this manuscript would be without her.

— TM
Winter 2022, New York City

About the Author

TERRY MCDONELL has published widely as a journalist, top-edited a number of magazines, and was elected to the American Society of Magazine Editors Hall of Fame in 2010. He is president *emeritus* of the Paris Review Foundation, and most recently cofounded Literary Hub.